THE ART OF THE POSSIBLE

THE ART
OF THE POSSIBLE

DIPLOMATIC ALTERNATIVES
IN THE MIDDLE EAST

MICHAEL REISMAN

PRINCETON UNIVERSITY PRESS
PRINCETON, NEW JERSEY

1970

This book has been composed in Linotype Granjon

Printed in the United States of America
by Princeton University Press

ACKNOWLEDGMENTS

I wish to acknowledge the comments and suggestions of my colleagues at the Yale Law School, Professors Myres S. McDougal, Harold D. Lasswell, Leon S. Lipson, and Eugene V. Rostow. Dr. Arieh E. David of the Faculty of Law of the Hebrew University of Jerusalem and Professor Richard A. Falk of Princeton University read and commented on earlier versions of the manuscript. Many of these men disagreed with parts of the work; none shares responsibility for what is said here. I was particularly fortunate in having the benefit of the editorial expertise and taste of Mr. Sanford G. Thatcher of Princeton University Press, and I owe him a special debt. The index was prepared by William L. Johnson. My wife Martha read and copyedited the work and helped in innumerable ways.

M. R.

New Haven, Connecticut
September 15, 1970

CONTENTS

THE ART OF THE POSSIBLE

INTRODUCTION

THE DAY-TO-DAY EVENTS transpiring in the Middle East are quickly and dramatically presented to the American public. What has been lost in the mundane montage of newsprint, radio, and television reports has been the larger view in which changing details become coherent, and in which proposed alternatives can be evaluated rationally. The aim of this book is to set a number of large problems, which converge on the Middle East, in a broad context, pointing up their complexity, but revealing the possibilities for positive and creative action. The opportunities afforded by periodic diplomatic efforts may well be squandered on false solutions if an appropriate frame of appraisal is not readily available.

Social life is considerably more complex than legal arithmetic. A political promise may seem to acquire its own discrete life; when the promise is broken, that life is terminated. But a promise, a treaty, a statute, or a statement of policy generates a pattern of behavior as individuals realign their lives in conformity to the expectation that has been created. When the promise ends, the behavior often continues and may even invoke the ruptured agreement as its own authority. The same events can be viewed by one group as past history, by another as daily life, and by a third as an expression of visionary change. This is the scrutable pattern of the Middle East. The outsider attempting to penetrate the Middle East finds himself in a multidimensional world in which past and present and, at times, an intensely demanded future coexist. History here is not archeological; it is psychological and social. Past empires and past policies have never been

[3]

uprooted; they have simply been covered by successors, while they themselves continued to exist in subtle behavior and thought patterns. There is barely an inch of the region whose title is not controverted by a number of claimants, each armed with unimpeachable documents culled at different points in time. If some of these claims invoke transempirical authority, there is scarcely a one that is not cogrounded or reinforced by the promises of a Western Power. The contemporary politics of the Middle East is, in many ways, a living museum of Western promises, duplicity, expediences, and the short memory of *Realpolitik*. If the first principle of knowledge about the region is that it exists in its own right, the corollary is that it has long been an extension and battleground of the West.

Wherever we commence—with Alexander of Macedon, the Crusades, Napoleon, or Disraeli—we have no difficulty in charting a steady flow of interest, manipulation, intervention, and colonization by the West in the East. The temporal, demographic, and geographic map of the region cannot be read without this understanding, and the minds and cultures of the peoples of the region cannot be fathomed without appreciating that the Middle East is *the* invaded civilization: it is the world's occupied territory par excellence. That Alexander is known in the West as "the Great" is an indication of the onesidedness of our historical perspective.

The Jews, a people with one of the oldest histories of suffering invasion and occupation, dispersed throughout the world and, in many places, continued to exist under oppressive conditions. About a century ago, a segment of European Jewry began to attempt some form of political realization of their ancient vision of a return to Zion. The earliest Zionist movement was an extremely complex and heterogeneous phenomenon, made up of religious elements, Jews whose orientation was cultural but not political, social radicals, and nationalists who, like the Young Finns and Young Turks, sought to fashion their own national symbols, barred as they were from participation in the febrile ethnic movements in Central and East Europe. The diverse groups slowly merged in a world organizational framework and gradually clarified a goal of a national home in Palestine.

The process of settling in Palestine began before the turn of the century and reproduced all the tensions and ambiguities that are always found in the encounter of groups—classes, cultures, generations—that have been shaped by decisively different experiences. The sharpness of division became accentuated, for as political Zionism refined its dogma, a young Arab intelligentsia was politicizing and nationalizing itself and experimenting with a variety of indigenous symbols of political organization. Among both Jews and Arabs, there were individuals who saw the opportunities of interstimulation and reciprocal enrichment and urged that integrative political institutions be fashioned. There were also intense exclusivists who viewed Arab or Jew, as the case was, as impediments, invaders, or agents of sinister external powers.

Pressures and ambitions on the Middle Eastern front in the First World War forced Great Britain to make complementary political promises to different groups as one way of gaining support in the war effort. Arab leaders in the urban centers, tribal sheikhs, and European and American Jewish community leaders were promised or given to understand that His Majesty's Government viewed with favor their particular aspirations and would, in appropriate circumstances, lend support. There is no point in undertaking an inventory of the promises or quasi-promises made, other than noting that, at best, they overlapped uncomfortably and that, at worst, they deeded outright the same property to contending parties. And with a peculiar half-life of their own, they continue to be factors in the Middle East equation.

The League of Nations' Palestine Mandate,* confirmed by the Council of the League on July 24, 1922, legitimated the effective control that Britain had been exercising in Palestine since Allenby occupied it in 1918. The document was replete with diplomatic ambiguities, which papered over most of the irreconcilable contradictions.

Democracies and bureaucracies are notoriously inefficient in handling problems that fall in the jurisdiction of more than one department; and most important problems unfortunately do. Conflicting promises and an erratic succession of policies from different government departments characterized British treatment of the Mandate during the interwar period. Whatever the political effect within Britain may have been, the result of these chiastic promises in Palestine was to reinforce the complementary expectations of the contending groups.

The rise of the Reich posed a crisis to all the parties involved, and once again vows of state were exchanged and broken in a dizzying pattern. But the most important effect of the Nazi accession to power was felt by the Zionists. The systematic destruction of European Jewry made the Zionist alternative entirely credible, and more

* For the text of the Mandate, see the Appendix, pp. 91ff.

and more Jews and sympathetic non-Jews came to support it. At the same time, Zionist leaders themselves were impelled to even greater efforts by the horrors they witnessed. The postwar period found a unique if momentary convergence of the interests of European governmental elites acting individually and in the United Nations, the Zionist organizations, displaced European Jews, and the Soviet Union, which gave international sanction to the establishment of a Jewish state. The Palestinian Arabs were less effectively represented, but were hardly forgotten. By 1947, as riots and disorder within Palestine were making it increasingly difficult for Britain to fulfill its obligations as Mandatory, the only plan presented to the United Nations that was acceptable to a majority of the members was one that provided for two separate states, one Palestinian and one Jewish, with certain institutionalized links between them. This plan was ultimately adopted by the United Nations and remains to date the most comprehensive and authoritative statement of international policy on the Arab-Jewish question.*

The plan was not accepted by the leaders of the Palestinian Arabs or by the surrounding Arab governments. In the war that ensued, Israel crystallized its boundaries, and perhaps over a million Arab inhabitants of Palestine† fled the Israeli territories, to become, for the most part, an ongoing responsibility of the world community. Overt hostilities came to an end with a series of bilateral armistice agreements. The Palestinian state was stillborn; Jor-

---

* For the text of the General Assembly's Resolution on the Future Government of Palestine, adopted on November 29, 1947, see the Appendix, pp. 100ff.

† On the problem of the number of Palestine refugees, see the "Comment" on pp. 58ff.

dan annexed its eastern section, an act in which Israel seems to have acquiesced, and Egypt took control of the Gaza Strip. There is no indication that any Arab government recognized the armistices to be anything approaching a peace system, though many Western governments found it convenient to construe the agreements and selected aspects of Arab behavior as constituting such recognition and as somehow binding the Arabs in the future. Individual Arab and Palestinian groups never felt so bound.

The successive Palestine wars have been interpreted as serial replays of the war of 1948-1949. They were more complex. The elite and thereafter the entire governmental structure of the Arab states began to change and has continued to change into the present. A Western-oriented aristocracy was systematically replaced by "Free Officers," of considerably lower social origins and with radically different social and political visions of both national and international affairs. As so often in the Arab world, Egypt took the initiative in this revolutionary venture; nationalization of the Suez Canal signalled an entirely new perspective in the Middle East situation and altered the course of regional and global politics irreversibly. Unfortunately, Western Powers had to fight and lose the first Sinai war before they began to appreciate the magnitude of the change.

The 1956 war involved three coordinating states, whose interests were separate, but whose instruments of realization happened to converge. Britain and France were concerned with control of the Suez Canal. Although Israel's access to the Canal might have been vouchsafed, her primary interest was to clear the Sinai Peninsula of organized and increasingly effective terrorist and paramilitary groups. The war of 1967, in contrast, revived the 1948 model, with new constraints introduced by parallel Russian and American commitments to each party.

Since 1967, Israel has retained control of three major Arab territories, ostensibly for bargaining purposes and for enhanced security. There has been no bargaining, and the security of the region has deteriorated steadily. The number of Palestinian refugees has swelled, and their condition has worsened. The level of armaments seems to be increasing exponentially, surpassed only by the rising level of fear and hate, driven deep into the younger generation. More money is being spent on military industry, whose product is destruction, and less on matters of social worth, whose product would be creation and amelioration. In the meantime, a shift in international ideology, reflected in the expanded membership of the United Nations, has grafted a completely new interpretation to the events of 1948: the self-determination of the Jewish people in 1948 has become, in 1970, the last bastion of European imperialism in the Middle East. With this change of ideological climate, much of the potential effectiveness of United Nations organs has been diminished. Responsible officials among the Great Powers have indicated that they share a terror of what can transpire, and from time to time in the past three years, they have sought to break out of the juggernaut. Unfortunately, the range of solutions considered has involved no more than minor variation on those complex circumstances that generated three fierce wars in less than twenty years. Unknowingly, our present peacemakers are programming the next war. The challenge to creative diplomacy is how to avoid it.

THE NAKED EMPERORS' CLUB

IN CONTEMPORARY WORLD POLITICS, there is a bizarre symbiosis in the relations between Great Powers and their vassals. Appearances notwithstanding, the Powers often lumber into positions in which the little fellows begin to call the tune and to pull the strings. This role inversion may already have occurred in the Middle East and in the alternately Two and Four Power Conference that seeks to solve the region's problems.

A strange hubris has come to overshadow the sporadic meetings of the Conference. It is widely assumed that if the Powers can only reach agreement among themselves, they will be able to impose a settlement or some form of lasting peace on the belligerents of the region. But short of invasion, long-term occupation, and extensive sociopolitical remodeling (all quite unthinkable), neither the United States nor the Soviet Union is capable of decisively influencing the outcome of events in the eastern Mediterranean; the ultimate dynamics of the region are not a reflection of Great Power struggles but are independent and, in many ways, autonomous. In the area itself, there is a symmetrical distortion. For millennia, Middle Easterners have construed their strife as the earthly counterpart of great divine or cosmic conflicts, and it is convenient and consistent with tradition to explain contemporary Mediterranean clashes in terms of good versus evil, capitalism versus communism, colonialism versus nationalism, and so on. But human conflict does not lie in the stars; it derives from much meaner and more accessible sources. The perspectives of Washington and Moscow are more childlike in their egocentricity: events acquire significance only insofar as they affect the power centers from which they are viewed, and events are part of reality only so long as the power centers continue to view them as such.

One hard look at the Middle East will see through these illusions. Each of the Great Powers has its protégés; by cutting off vital supplies, each can cause its current vassal to postpone objectives or to change strategies, perhaps even to shop for a new protector. But no more than this. The nuclear powers are simply musclebound. They are overequipped in "fate control"—the capacity to decide whether or not to obliterate the region—and underequipped in "behavior control"—the capacity to influence, in a significant and lasting way, the political actions of Israel and the Arab states.* Power relations are always complex and are remarkably reciprocal. Without a deep psychological submission, supremacy is always temporary; even with such submission, it is relative. The grandest power is whittled by distance, by time, by crisis, by the inexorable demands for cooperation, and, often, by its own overextension.

We have enormously magnified the influence-potential of the Russians over Syria and Egypt; the Russians, for their part, seem to have evolved a complementary view of our ability to influence Israel. In fact, there is no evidence that the Soviet Union has constrained Egypt to do anything which it would not have done in any case. For

* J. Thibaut and H. Kelley, *The Social Psychology of Groups* (New York: John Wiley & Sons, 1959).

all their efforts, the Russians did not succeed in preventing President Nasser from initiating the June war.* The American press has recorded that it is feverish Soviet diplomatic activity that has since kept Nasser from launching a second, equally suicidal bout. But it is just as plausible to construe the situation contrariwise. Nasser may well realize that he is not in a position to undertake a successful follow-up war; the dense presence of Russians in Cairo have permitted him to be a verbal militant and, at the same time, to blame a short Soviet leash for his relative inactivity. The more violent his rhetoric, the more nervous the Russians have become and the more anxious to extend even further their ruble and MIG diplomacy. It requires no small amount of credulousness to believe that a promise made to Mr. Kosygin would deter President Nasser from starting another war when he thinks that circumstances are ripe.

If there is a single factor that now influences President Nasser or, for that matter, any erstwhile moderate in the Arab camp, it is the spokesmen for the most extreme position. Effective political propaganda ultimately captures the propagandist himself; and once the dogmatic

* A devil theory, evolved in a number of Western capitals, holds that the June war was set off by Russian black intelligence, which the Soviet Union concocted and circulated in order to initiate the hostilities. One gloss on this theory contends that the Russians wished the Arabs to lose in order to open the way for further Soviet penetration in the region! These theories stretch credibility to the breaking point. It is one thing to impute to the Russians actions that raised the crisis-level in the region; it is quite another to suggest that the Russians wanted hot war of *any* kind there with *any* outcome. A closer examination of Soviet interests in the region will show that Russia requires very severe limits to Middle Eastern conflict.

frame of mind is insulated from compromise with adversaries, it is thoroughly vulnerable to a more dogmatic position, precisely because it has been inculcated with dogma. It is neither Israel nor the United States that hardens or softens the heart of Pharaoh; it is Mr. Arafat and, increasingly, his own extremist fleas.

American relations with Israel are roughly symmetrical to Russian relations with Egypt. The United States was not successful in forestalling an Israeli preemptive strike on the morning of June 5, 1967, nor has American pressure deterred Israel from effective annexation of the Old City of Jerusalem or from retaliatory strikes in response to commando incursions. An arms embargo or limitation of specified items to Israel cannot seriously change the power balance, if all the factors of military competence are taken into consideration. Even an embargo on jet planes and parts would not turn Israel from a course of action it judged to be vital for its survival. The Israelis have proved themselves to be a remarkably resourceful people; it is difficult to imagine that they have failed to develop alternatives for just this sort of contingency. This is not to suggest that the Israelis do not incorporate projected extra-regional responses in the formulation of their own policy: they patently do. What it does mean is that Israel, like Egypt, is unlikely to be coerced into doing something it deems to be against its interests. It may, however, be influenced to adopt policies conducive to its interests, it may be persuaded to view its interests in a different light, and it may be presented with new "package" interests that include components provided by states outside the region.

United States and Soviet Interests

Regional violence need not acquire global dimensions. There are scattered pockets about the globe in which small wars grind on; they have only immediate local significance precisely because the major Powers, through either neglect or choice, do not transform them into proxy wars. To an extent, this has been the essence of an unenunciated and perhaps reluctant Big Power consensus in the Middle East since 1948. The states of the Fertile Crescent have been permitted to fight and to make minor border rearrangements, on the condition that the established political entities be maintained. The moment major changes have been asserted or the existence of one of the states has appeared to be in jeopardy, the Power that had designated itself protector has indicated that it might be obliged to intervene. Hence, rough boundaries to the scope of conflict have been sustained: maintenance of established entities and tolerated local conflict short of Superpower intervention and confrontation. The unanimous Resolution* of the Security Council of November 22, 1967—the world's major policy statement regarding the Middle East since the June war—is simply a detailed reiteration of what has been, for all practical purposes, the shared policy of the Powers. Significantly, the difficulties of implementation have not derived from the United States and the Soviet Union; they have come from the local states themselves.

In the course of two years, the uneasy cease-fire of June 12, 1967, has deteriorated into what United Nations Secretary-General U Thant now calls "open war." This

---

* For the text of the Resolution, see the Appendix, pp. 157-58.

trend of events is neither surprising nor inconsistent with the Superpower consensus. A First-World-War, "Western"-style front on the Suez Canal is only a difference of degree. If the Powers are able to restrain the local combatants from trying to push each other back, the Suez line may be maintained indefinitely. Unfortunately, they cannot; Suez is an unstable border for several reasons. Having begun to recruit its army from the city rather than from the still preindustrial countryside, Egypt has reached the "take-off point" of garrison statehood: it can continue to mobilize, but it cannot demobilize without serious economic dislocation and probably political revolution. As mobilization continues, the military machine acquires an autochthonous dynamic that can rush it into hopeless war. And even before this point is reached, Israel, stung by Egyptian provocations, may cross Suez and bring the war to the enemy. Israel, for its part, is rapidly tooling itself into a significant military manufacturer and supplier. It will, reportedly, manufacture a French prototype jet within two years and its own supersonic fighter-bomber before the decade ends. Overlooking for the moment the very real possibility of a *qualitative* change in weaponry, it is increasingly clear that Israel itself may generate a war dynamic if its own continuing sense of insecurity is not assuaged now. Deflecting the Egyptian and Israeli trends will require innovative thinking within and outside of the Middle East. And it will require cooperation.

It is an idiosyncrasy of international law and international relations as well as of the mass-media web of communications that primary focus is placed upon conflict. In fact, contemporary international relations, viewed comprehensively, manifest much more cooperation than is appreciated. In vast areas of international exchange, there is effective and stabilized interaction; and even limited conflict must be premised upon broad agreement on the parameters to which hostility will be limited. American-Russian relations, for example, are a peculiar blend of conflict and collaboration. In the Middle East, the United States and the Soviet Union each pursue—or at least believe that the other pursues—a hostile policy incompatible with its own; successful realization of the other's policy, it is believed, would cause an intolerable imbalance of power. Hence, there is conflict within severe limits. If the entire system is costly, it is nonetheless worthwhile, in terms of the strange, indeed absurd, logic of international politics, so long as other vital interests are not jeopardized and broader, unlimited conflict is prevented.*

In the Middle Eastern situation, the regional dynamic over which the Powers have no control is eroding the

---

* Indeed, superficial conflicts in the Middle East, which have persuaded many official and private observers of the ultimate incompatibility of Russian and American interests in the region, may conceal a very deep identity. By championing the Egyptian cause, the Soviet Union has become a proponent of Pan-Arab union, while the United States has been pressed into the position of being an opponent of this program. Official American policy has been to provide peoples about the globe with the opportunity to determine their own destiny; this has sometimes entailed the support of vigorous local nationalisms where they have emerged, as they have in the Middle East. Yet it is a test of credulity to believe that the Soviet Union would really like a united Arab nation of one hundred million, sitting on its border from Batum to Seraks. It is more reasonable to assume that the Soviet Union would prefer a fractionated Arab world, with as much contact with the West (and East) as Stalin permitted Eastern Europe!

boundaries of the conflict and now threatening vital interests shared by the United States, the Western nations, and the Soviet Union in a variety of ways. The most obvious interest endangered is the use of the Suez Canal. For the Socialist states, closure of the Canal represents an impediment to interlocking political and trade goals. The political objectives of Western Europe and the United States in East Africa and the Far East are quite different from those of the Soviet Union. But they are, nevertheless, affected by the state of the Canal. Western commercial and trade stakes in the Canal are even greater. And, obversely, various Asian states in whose development the West has taken a considerable interest are undergoing severe transportation difficulties because of the Canal's blockage.*

A second shared interest now threatened is control of the arms race and weapons escalation. It is no secret that Israel is a prime candidate for membership in the nuclear weapons club, and it is only wishful to imagine that Israel

---

* Paradoxically, Israel itself has an urgent interest in continued world use of the Suez Canal *even if it continues to be barred from the Canal*. If the Canal remains closed for an extended period, world shipping may accommodate itself to the fact by building technologically innovative fleets that render the Canal superfluous. Should trade routes crystallize around the Cape, the international status of the Straits of Aqaba and the Red Sea may come into doubt. The Arab League is already preparing documents to establish these seas as historic Arab waters subject to joint Arab control. And there are indeed precedents in international law for such a gambit. One guarantee for Israeli shipping through Aqaba and the Red Sea is the continuing intense global demand for the international status of these waters. This demand is contingent on continuing Western maritime perception of the indispensability of the Canal. Such a perception perforce wanes each additional day the Canal remains closed.

will not take that step if its perception of gross insecurity continues. It is difficult to believe that the United Arab Republic will not follow suit. The lid of Pandora's box will be completely opened. Such a sequence would involve the radical restructuring not only of a regional arena but of the entire world arena. This clearly runs counter to shared American-Russian policy. The continuing high level of insecurity in the Middle East may also undermine the wobbling restraints on the use of chemical and gas weapons, the contemporary bargain basement of sophisticated armaments.

These developments threaten a material confrontation of the Great Powers in the Middle East and underline the failure of the consensus strategy in this region. In terms of game structure and bargaining theory, the pattern of consensus in the Middle East can work only if no local participant, with objectives different from those of the Great Powers, is in a position to start another war, involving all and terminating in what gamers fear the most: a "final score" and the end of the game. But now this is precisely what can too palpably happen. In short, the consensus cannot work. The dramatic poses and windy rhetoric that have been used to camouflage the persisting consensus among the Powers no longer provide even an illusion of control. Much more must be done, and it is in the interest of both the Soviet Union and the United States to do it. Yet the limited influence-potential of the Powers seems to bar both agreement and implementation.

A New Perspective

As the belligerents and powers move toward detailed negotiations, it is obvious that a radically different perspective is required and that new, more realistic, and more achievable goals must be formulated. As a matter of policy, we must quite seriously ask ourselves what ought to be done, and as a matter of practical politics, we must dispassionately determine what can be done. Diplomats and lawyers regularly respond to crisis situations by invoking the mystical nostrum of status quo ante. Where the circumstances of the past indicate with cyclical eloquence that they regularly degenerate into violence, it is hardly wise diplomacy to return to them. Unfortunately, this seems to be the agenda for the Middle East.

Insofar as there is shared commitment to breaking out of the vicious circle of Middle Eastern war, four major revisions must be made immediately. *First*, the proclaimed goal of "peace" should cede its place to one of minimum order. With or without Israel, the Middle East is and will remain a volatile arena, ambivalent to all outsiders and, in particular, suspicious of Western Europe and the United States. There are enough flaring conflicts of ambition between the elites of the different Arab states to insure continuing unrest and violence in that region for years to come. In these circumstances, the realistic challenge is to secure some system of minimum order, which at once permits Israeli existence, Arab social and economic development, and the participation of the East and the West in their crossroads.

Second, the assumption of the monolithic or integrated nature of the problems of the Middle East must be reexamined. Participants within the region as well as many states outside it have assumed, as a matter of course, that there is a single problem with two adversaries: the Arabs and the Israelis. Influenced by the rhetoric of Pan-

Islam and by the identity of language and cultural heritage among the Arab states, we have come to assume that there must be a single, encompassing answer to a single, encompassing problem. But a problem is formulated by the problem-solver; depending upon the facts and policies involved, the problems in the Middle East can be integrated or fractionated. The need for "packagism" is, of course, recognized by the Powers and by many of the Middle Eastern states themselves; yet even this notion often assumes that the same essential problem is recurring in a number of different fronts and contexts. In fact, the situation in the Middle East is composed of a variety of separate issues, many of which converge with Israel, but each of which requires a separate approach and a distinct diplomatic strategy: the relations between Israel and Egypt, between Israel and Syria, between Israel, Jordan, and the Palestinian Arab people, and the status of Jerusalem. Each of these four problems has a different history, involves different political and moral factors, and is susceptible to a different solution. Securing *peace* in the Middle East is as difficult as securing it anywhere else in the world. But creating the groundwork for a system of minimum order may be possible, if separate problems are identified.

Third, the ambiguous rhetoric of "imposed" versus "indigenous" solutions must be scrapped, for it forces a complex reality of great diplomatic potential into a disjunctive frame of macabre distortion. The semantic contents of words like "imposed" and "indigenous" vary depending on who is using them. As a practical matter, outsiders are involved to the hilt, *on all sides*, in the contemporary struggle. Any group that finds the immediate and feasibly projected circumstances to its net advantage describes the situation as an expression of the indigenous participants; it conveniently overlooks the extent to which external power is responsible for the situation, while stigmatizing any changes in external involvement as impositions and interventions. Any group that finds the immediate and feasibly projected circumstances to its net disadvantage simply reverses the labels.

The Middle East has been and will continue to be a crossroads of North and South as well as East and West; all social entities that are engaged in any interchange along these routes are involved in the Middle East. No one can gainsay the prominent role of local participants in the formation of the current situation and, prospectively, in the establishment of general conditions of noncoercive minimum order. By the same token, no one can fail to recognize the crucial supporting and at times initiating role of other states in creating *and sustaining* the contemporary status quo. The unique geographical situation of the Middle East as well as the more general circumstances of transnational interaction and the interdependence of all states of the world means that there can be no such thing as a strictly "imposed" or strictly "indigenous" solution. Every putative solution and every stabilization short of solution will be one in which regional and extra-regional entities participate. And the viability of any proposed solution will depend on the degree to which it provides minimum order and the opportunity for productive collaboration of all those concerned about the region.

Fourth, the need for social and political invention must be recognized without qualification. The space age has introduced us to radically new and in many ways humbling conceptions of time and space. In comparison with the awesome vastness of solar time, the five or six millennia of recorded human history constitute a ludicrously short period and provide an extremely limited storehouse of human experience. That shard of past history that we do have contains almost no successful models for dealing with racial and ethnic conflict. Atavistic inclinations in the search for solutions will doom the entire enterprise to failure. We require an unfettered investigation of new political techniques and legal institutions, tooled to goals of minimum order and the particular exigencies of the context in which they must be realized. The inevitable carping criticism, "this has never been done," may be a milestone informing us that we are on the right path.

EGYPT AND SINAI

THE STATE SYSTEM of the Middle East is a relatively recent creation, formed in part after the First World War, but coming fully into operation as a more or less independent system only after World War II. It is a multipolar arena and will exhibit the realignment processes and consequent tensions characteristic of such an arena whether or not the state of Israel exists. Egypt, or the United Arab Republic as it now styles itself, has emerged as the mini-Superpower of the region; its policies of expansion and incorporation under the guises of Pan-Arabism and Pan-Islam have been a destabilizing influence, which can be expected to continue even if Israel is struck from the map. Part of the United Arab Republic's drive may stem from a missionary tradition that has conceived Egypt as the cultural and spiritual *entrepot* for all Arabdom. But the primary impetus at present seems to derive from the governmental structure of Egypt.

Since Farouk's overthrow and Naguib's accession to power, the officer corps has composed the political elite and the primary base of power of any politician. In return for its political support, the Army has made heavy demands upon incumbent leaders for prestige within the country as well as for the most advanced and sophisticated military equipment. This is hardly an unusual phenomenon in developing countries, and as Latin American (if not our own) experience demonstrates, the demand of a military-political complex for more of the latest, sophisti-

cated, and prestigious equipment proceeds without necessary relation to the security needs (if any) of the state.

Barring a major restructuring of the Egyptian government, the United Arab Republic will continue to follow
this pattern. There is no indication that peace with or the
destruction of Israel will alter it. And as long as the military maintains its position of political preeminence, the
demand for weapons will be unceasing. If Egypt does not
acquire nuclear weapons, it will not be because of the
eradication of Israel or because of a tacit agreement with
Israel to refrain reciprocally from taking this step. Rather,
it will result from a combination of internal incapacity
and frantic external pressure (coming at the present time
primarily from the Soviet Union). And these may prove
to be insufficient checks.

A Middle East arms race of conventional magnitude
will continue, without regard to the Israeli question, for
other reasons. Some states are more war-prone than others,
either because of internal dynamics, geographical obses-
sions, or ideological compulsions. In particular, the
infiltration of civic government by officers who retain
their military identity seems to diminish psychological
restraints and to increase the propensity for the use of
arms as a diplomatic instrument and for its own sake.
Egypt is a case in point—and not, unfortunately, the
exclusive one in the Middle East. It is not only militaristic
vis-à-vis Israel but has been bent on military engagement
in a variety of confrontations. In the 1950's, the possibility
of war flared with the Sudan and with Libya. Threats
have constantly been directed at Jordan, whose defense
forces have been mobilized to provide protection against
other Arab states as much as (and perhaps more than)

against Israel. In 1963, Egypt created its own little Vietnam in Yemen and carried on a campaign noteworthy for the absence of even the minimum restraints of modern warfare. And, of course, the major threat to Saudi Arabia, from the Saudis' point of view and probably from Washington's, continues to be Egypt. Egypt's interest in Iran and ambitions in the Persian Gulf are no secret. If further proof of militaristic impetuosity is needed, consider the ill-prepared initiation of a suicidal war with Israel in June of 1967. Any diplomatic assessment of the Middle East that identifies Israel as the exclusive or even major canker and cause of instability in the region is hallucination.

At the moment, of course, the core diplomatic challenge is Egyptian-Israeli relations and, in particular, the disposition of the Sinai Peninsula. But in attempting to fashion a solution to this particular problem, it is crucial that the creative diplomat grasp that he is faced with only one manifestation of a persisting condition caused in greatest part by social, economic, and political circumstances within Egypt. Any effective and lasting solution must treat not only the symptoms on the Egyptian-Israeli malapropian "cease-fire" line but also the causes within Egypt. The durability of a solution on the Sinai front will turn, in no small measure, on the degree to which it ameliorates the major problems within Egypt. Insofar as a solution satisfies this desideratum, it may also be expected to resolve a variety of other latent conflicts toward which Egypt may be heading.

The current importance of Sinai is geopolitical. It is almost totally uninhabited and potentially inhabitable only at an expense beyond the capacities of local states.

It does not appear to be exceptionally abundant in natural resources; in any case, the exploitation of Sinai resources was never a crucial strut in the Egyptian economy, nor has it been such in the Israeli economy in the last two years. Since June of 1967, the Egyptians' most urgent concern has been the return of Sinai. Egypt would probably submit to some regime of neutralization for the area as the price of its return and possibly even promise Israel unrestricted use of the Suez Canal. In the light of past Egyptian behavior, neither promise would be very credible. Israel's legitimate interest in Sinai is security. It is doubtful that any Israeli politician would urge relinquishment of control of Sinai without an effective neutralization regime. Given the current strength and political alignments of the United Nations, no effective or acceptable neutralization scheme is feasible without detailed and credible Superpower support.

Professor Nadav Safran, in a recent publication,* has identified the disposition of Sinai as a pivotal problem and a key to peace in the region. Professor Safran hews to a monolithic conception of Middle Eastern problems and believes that if an agreement can be purchased with Egypt, the other Arab belligerents will fall into line. The gravamen of Egypt's bellicosity, according to Safran, has not been Israel as such, but rather Israel as a geographical wedge acting as a land barrier to Nasser's Pan-Arab ambitions. Hence, Professor Safran suggests a lateral division of Sinai that would permit Egypt direct contact with Jordan and Saudi Arabia but would leave Israel a corridor extending to the Suez Canal, insuring the freedom of its

* "The Alternatives in the Middle East," *Commentary*, May 1969.

shipping and providing it, in effect, with a dagger at Egyptian vitals—ready access to Cairo. Once the road is clear for Nasser's march to a Pan-Arab state, Safran believes, Israel will cease to be a target.

Even assuming that the crux of Nasser's animus against Israel is its location, the basic question for the Powers is not resolved. Will satisfying Nasser's minimum condition really provide the groundwork for a minimum system of order in the Middle East? Probably not. There are no grounds for equating Nasser's vision of Pan-Arabism with Arab nationalism. Egyptian experience in Syria, Yemen, Jordan, and among the Palestinian commandos has shown that there is a vigorous nationalism in each of these states that can struggle quite effectively against Egyptian attempts at suzerainty. That Nasser's picture is prominently displayed at public functions throughout the Arab world no more betokens a popular desire to become part of Egypt than did the display of Stalin's picture in China in the fifties mean that Chairman Mao's secret passion was to make China a province of the Union of Soviet Socialist Republics.

There is a tremendous gap between President Nasser's Arabist ambitions and those of the elites and people of the neighboring Arab countries. There is no reason, in principle or in *Realpolitik*, for the West to commit itself to aiding Nasser in his ambition. Perhaps because of our own federal experience, perhaps because of a cultural or esthetic drive for monism, perhaps because of deep psychological drives, even the most democratic of our citizens often responds with awe to the imperial ambitions of others if they are decked out in the proper symbols. But unity between disparate political entities is sought in order to realize certain policies. In different contexts and at different times, unity is not always the appropriate instrument. And even where it is, the governmental credentials of the self-selected unifier should be carefully scrutinized. Nasser's Pan-Arabism, no less than Sukarno's abortive Mahapajit empire and Nkrumah's Pan-Africanism, is a vision of personal imperialism, and not popular development. There is no moral reason why we should jump on any of these bandwagons. And morality aside, there is no political payoff in it. Even at the apogee of their power, none of these putative empire-builders had the capacity to realize his ambitions, only to stir trouble and provoke violent reactions. Neither the United States nor the Soviet Union stands to gain from Arab internecine warfare, for each has interests in and commitments to a number of different Arab states and might find itself seriously implicated in any conflict.

What interests are shared by the United States and the Soviet Union in this area? From a practical political standpoint, returning the Sinai Peninsula to Egypt is not the pressing matter. The urgent items on the world agenda are, first, securing an effective cease-fire on the Suez front; second, opening the Canal to general maritime use; and third, creating conditions, insofar as is possible, persuasive, and economical, that would halt Egypt's expansion into the Middle East.

Several months after the Sinai war, it might have been possible for Israel to accomplish these objectives by unilaterally announcing its willingness to allow Egypt to dredge and reopen the Canal, even withdrawing a limited distance from its bank. Presumably, there would have been intense pressure exerted on Egypt by all states depending upon maritime transit to resume Canal operations. The Canal, functioning as an international waterway, would have created a *de facto* boundary, and Egypt would probably have been loath to jeopardize the operation of the Canal and the consequent flow of revenues by conducting commando raids and artillery duels offering dubious military and political gains. This solution is less feasible now; with monthly allowances from Saudi Arabia and Kuwait and with the vast resources of Libya available, the urgency of the United Arab Republic's need for the Suez Canal as a source of foreign exchange has, at least for the present, diminished. And in the future a Sinai-type situation may be resolved by a vast program of geoarchitecture, perhaps a "plowshares" project cutting a thirty-mile maritime belt through Sinai from the Mediterranean to the Gulf of Aqaba.* Solutions of this sort, which are not presently feasible, would create a durable buffer between Egypt and Israel, on the one hand, and between Egypt and Jordan and Egypt and Saudi Arabia, on the other. They would not, however, affect or alter the underlying tensions causing the conflict.

In place of these radical projects, an effective form of

* This is an exhortation to a pattern of thinking and not to the implementation of a particular recommendation. Any projects to alter the face of Sinai would have to consider the aggregate of probable effects on the entire socioenvironmental context. Although the technology for accomplishing many such feats of physical transformation is available, a comprehensive contextual model for assessing the interrelated biospheric changes is not; it is an urgent priority. On the other hand, it is not too early to begin to consider planned environmental changes for shared political goals. The capacity to intervene in natural processes and to force nature to discriminate in favor of man has major political as well as nutritional ramifications.

neutralization of Sinai must be achieved. The neutralization will have to be politically and economically attractive enough to secure Egyptian agreement to a formal diminution of its sovereignty in the Sinai Peninsula and to insure continued Egyptian acceptance of such a regime and, at the same time, be credible enough to persuade Israel to accept it and to withdraw from the Canal zone. Credibility will derive from a number of factors: the palpable political and economic advantage of the neutralization scheme to the Egyptian economy, and the severe economic consequences that would ensue for Egypt were the neutralization scheme to end.

A Sinai Development Trust

One technique for effective neutralization of Sinai might be the creation of an externally supervised "Sinai Development Trust," applying a vast scheme of development to the Sinai Peninsula. The SDT would be an international or global corporation, capitalized by investments from the United States and the Soviet Union as well as from all the states of the Middle East; other nonregional states would be encouraged to contribute. Investments would be in the form of bonds rather than shares, in order to emphasize the decisional independence of the SDT. The Board of Trustees of SDT would be composed of international civil servants, private individuals, and representatives of the regional states. The Board would operate independently of any state, but its operations would be annually audited by the International Monetary Fund or the World Bank. In addition to its initial capitalization, the SDT could float further bond issues in national markets.

The United Arab Republic would grant a fifty-year exclusive concession to the SDT for the purpose of undertaking the development of Sinai.* Egyptian nationals would, of course, be employed at all levels of the Trust, but in the final ten years of the SDT's life span, Egyptians would systematically replace all foreign nationals in the higher echelons of management, so that, at the moment of termination, the return of full authority to Egypt would only be a formality and would in no way affect the operation of the Trust. There would be no question of Egypt's residual sovereignty over the Sinai Peninsula; however, agreements of predetermined categories (as set out in the SDT's statute) would be deemed to bind Egypt after termination of the Trust. Contracts to supply surrounding states with fresh water, electricity, or certain minerals, for example, would survive the SDT. On the other hand, the SDT would not be authorized to conclude any agreements whose span would extend more than twenty-five years beyond its own termination. This balance would at once guarantee a high measure of regional stability and yet avoid any perpetual encumbrance of the United Arab Republic's rights over its territory.

For the duration of the SDT, no Egyptian military forces or police forces would be permitted in Sinai. Routine police functions and border supervision would be carried out by an SDT police force of a multinational character. A special jurisdictional agreement would pro-

---

* There is nothing magical in the symbol fifty. The point is to create an expectation of a period of time in which there is a realistic probability of development; as one consequence, the expectation of an effective political buffer in Sinai should appreciate. If any other number or numerical formula fulfills these goals and perhaps others more effectively, it should be substituted.

vide for trial of Egyptian employees in Egyptian courts. Non-Egyptian nationals accused of offenses would be extradited to their own states for trial and, upon conviction, punishment. Initial determinations of "probable cause" for extradition would be made by SDT magistrates.

Every signatory to the SDT statute would enjoy a right to lodge claims against the SDT or against other signatories for alleged violations of the statute. A special jurisdictional agreement would allow immediate hearings by the International Court of Justice, which would render final decisions in the disputes.

The SDT itself would probably not engage in direct development projects but, instead, would grant subconcessions and licenses for periods of less than fifty years and restrict itself to supervisory functions. Different national corporations might tender development proposals, and joint enterprises of foreign companies and Egyptian companies could be expected. There is no reason why Israeli investment groups could not compete. Crucial infrastructural projects, however, might demand a higher degree of SDT supervision or active enterprise. A nuclear power plant, for example, harnessed to water purification and electrical production, might be run jointly by the SDT and the International Atomic Energy Agency. Workers' housing might be closely supervised by the SDT and the International Labour Organization; education, by the SDT and UNESCO; and so on.

For an extended period of time, the profits of the SDT would be required to service and amortize the various bond issues floated. Thereafter, profits might be reinvested in new SDT projects. When, later in the lifespan of the SDT, profits did accrue, they would be placed in a special account in the World Bank to the credit of the United Arab Republic. The account would become payable to Egypt only on termination of the SDT. Prior to termination, it would be available, through the jurisdictional scheme, to claimants who could establish Egyptian breaches of the SDT statute.

A conventional economic inventory of the development possibilities of Sinai might misinterpret some of its features as debits when they are really potential assets. Because Sinai has been a vast wilderness, planners may arrange the most rational situational relations of people, resources, and innovative behavior without dislocating a settled population. The opportunity for industrial and demographic preplanning may allow for optimum integration of nuclear energy plants in production cycles; existing demographic patterns in industrialized societies have tended to prevent such optimal use. That there is nothing in Sinai at the moment other than a political and economic need for industrialization has other beneficial dimensions. Our technical and industrial capacity seems to be at a new take-off point, in which integrated systems conceptions promise the greatest return. Obviously, such systems must be built from the ground up; Sinai offers this possibility. Consider the production of nuclear energy. One by-product, currently treated (at great expense) as a waste, is heat. In an integrated SDT system, heat might be viewed, not as a waste, but as a thermal resource that could be exploited in another industrial process in a different section of the Peninsula.

If the Middle East is taken as a developmental construct, the location of Sinai can itself be a major resource. As a peninsula, with easy ocean access to North and East

Africa, South Asia, Western Europe, and Eastern Europe via the Bosporus, Sinai is the real juncture of North, South, East, and West. The SDT can draw on the resources of any of these sectors and, in return, deliver resources and finished and semi-finished products of its own. As its level of industrialization rises, its function as a political buffer appreciates. As external investment in Sinai mounts, the external interest in preventing a Sinai or trans-Sinai war grows.

Shared Benefits of the SDT

Effective implementation of an SDT necessarily requires the minimum cooperation of Israel, Egypt, and the Powers. And this cooperation can only arise from perceived benefits. Israel, Jordan, and Saudi Arabia would gain in the SDT the demilitarization and neutralization of Sinai. All of these states and the United States and Soviet Union as well would benefit by a reduction of Egyptian influence in the rest of the Middle East. As the development program of the SDT was realized, a multiplier effect would be experienced in the entire region, and all would share in the rewards. And there would be political bounties to be had, too. Each day the SDT developed, its economic value to the United Arab Republic—the primary beneficiary of the plan—would increase the *deterrent* potential of Sinai on any Egyptian ambitions in the region. For the SDT, unlike a complex such as Aswan, could hardly escape being the first casualty in any Israeli-Egyptian confrontation. Paradoxically, Israel's greatest security from Egyptian belligerency lies not in Egyptian underdevelopment, but rather in radical Egyptian industrialization. By its location, Sinai, industralized, would provide maximum deterrence.

An SDT promises major gains to the United Arab Republic. First, and most obvious, Egypt would regain Sinai. This is a prospect with very little certainty at present, and one that could be realized coercively only with exceedingly high costs. Second, Egypt would gain an international buffer. Whether or not Egyptian elites actually believe that Israel represents an expansionist threat—at certain levels of consciousness, some may entertain this notion—the Egyptian rank and file have been fed this image and seem to have digested it thoroughly. Because their constituents are imbued with this belief, no Egyptian government can accede to a plan that does not seem defensively sound. The SDT would be an extraordinary defense, and its credibility would increase in proportion to the amount of foreign capital invested in Sinai. With each additional dollar, ruble, pound, and franc invested in the Sinai Peninsula, the states of the world would themselves become increasingly mortgaged to a policy of peace and stability in the region.

The scale of investment of capital and skill in the SDT would be unmatched in history. Any governmental elite genuinely committed to social and economic development would be hard pressed to justify refusal of such a plan. And the form of development would be particularly unobtrusive in the political sense. Sinai has been virtually uninhabited and on the farthest periphery of almost all aspects of Egyptian society. The areas of relatively dense population on the east bank of the Suez Canal could be formally excluded from the SDT and returned to full

Egyptian suzerainty. They are, in any case, geographically contiguous with metropolitan Egypt.

With the SDT providing a buffer, the Suez Canal could be reopened and its revenues harvested once again, and Egyptian resources could be concentrated in metropolitan and upper Egypt, the latter a seriously underdeveloped region. At the same time, the Cairo region, which suffers from chronic unemployment and underemployment, would find a job market in the SDT and in secondary Egyptian industries that would grow to serve the increased demand created by SDT activities. Finally, a developed Sinai would dwarf the pyramids as the greatest legacy a group of political leaders have ever bequeathed their nation.

Whatever the final disposition of their claims, the Palestinian Arabs stand to gain by the SDT. In Gaza, where several hundred thousand Palestinians have subsisted for more than twenty years, there is no industry, and as a result there has been a disastrous level of unemployment. The SDT, by its proximity, would provide an abundant source of gainful employment. International funds that have been channeled through the United Nations for refugee aid could be used for specific training and even for the establishment of cooperative enterprises, owned and run by the Gaza residents.

For the United States and the Soviet Union, a crucial flashpoint that has threatened to engulf them could be permanently neutralized, without charges of a sellout and without ensuing danger to their contraposed protégés. All states would benefit by a reopening of the Suez Canal. Whether or not Israel was to regain its right to passage through the Canal would be a matter for negotiation, which might be profitably deferred for at least five years when, in a cooler political climate, chances for successful agreement might be improved. For all the political rhetoric expended, Israeli passage was not a vital question. Passage through the Canal is of utility to all maritime states and would obviously be beneficial to Israel. But Israel has survived and flourished without it for twenty years, and international, non-Egyptian control of Sinai and, in particular, of Sharm el Sheikh by the SDT would insure it access to the Red Sea and the Indian Ocean from the port of Elath.

Sequence of Implementation

The steps in implementing the SDT become secondary (albeit technically complex) once those states affected by it perceive their common interest in a drastic change of the Sinai front. First and most important is a recognition by the United States and the Soviet Union that they share an urgent interest in it. This will not easily be accomplished, but it can be done, as the Test Ban Treaty and the Non-Proliferation Convention demonstrate. Once this consensus has been reached, each Power must undertake to persuade its protégé. The most effective Superpower threat vis-à-vis Egypt is the implicit possibility that the Powers will simply reduce the intensity of the demand for repatriation of Sinai and, by their nonfeasance, stabilize and buttress Israeli control of the Peninsula.

A frequently anticipated impediment to any flexible maneuvering by the Egyptian elite has been that it would involve jettisoning one of the basic legitimizations of power in the United Arab Republic: anti-Zionism. Implementation of the SDT certainly imports forswearing militant anti-Zionism, in theory and in practice. Yet it does not mean that President Nasser or his successor must deck himself out in blue and white stripes and six-pointed stars. There is a vast spectrum between the poles of love and hate; there is no reason why Egypt could not assume an attitude toward Israel roughly equivalent to that taken by the United States toward Yugoslavia. Indeed, Cecil Hourani has long sought to persuade Arabs that this is the safest and most economic way of absorbing Israel.* Nor is it certain that all or even most Egyptians are anti-Israel (or for that matter Arabists, let alone Pan-Arabists). There is no shortage of examples of modern political parties changing their substantive programs by emphasizing different symbols. In Israel, Mapai has done this, moving rapidly from a program of comparatively pristine socialism to one of enterprise, welfare, and bureaucracy. Even more to the point is the example of India's Jan Sangh, transmogrifying itself from an anti-Moslem Hindu party to one courting Moslem membership! (In so doing, it might be added, Jan Sangh has become a party of real political significance in India.)

Influencing Israeli thought on the SDT must be based on other considerations, many of which are quite independent of Superpower behavior. Israel's public stance in the Middle East has, since 1948, been nonexpansionist; control, as opposed to annexation of Sinai, is justifiable only so long as a palpable security consideration remains paramount. A power-backed SDT proposal would offer a realistic alternative and change, in one stroke, defensive Israeli control of Sinai into an act of expansion and aggres-

* See, for example, "The Moment of Truth," *Encounter*, Nov. 1967.

[38]

sion. Israeli elites and rank and file would be reluctant
to be dragged into such a development.

Ultimately, it will be the cost of retaining Sinai that
will impel Israel to seek alternatives to neutralization.
Israeli technocrats certainly have already considered the
resource value and exploitation potential of Sinai; mid-
level governmental initiatives of this sort develop an
autonomous dynamic, fueled by a built-in governmental
pressure group, which can be expected to tout the tactical,
economic, and even religious advantages of holding Sinai.
But Egyptian intransigence over surrendering its patrimony has already shown that the cost for Israel is a garrison state and a painfully regular loss of life. Israeli voters,
one hopes, are too sophisticated to buy desert at this price.

The process of diplomatic persuasion may be accelerated by overlapping it with third-party initiation of some
of the technical features of the program. In addition to
reinforcing international commitment to the SDT, actually commencing the project can persuade those whose
imagination has been decisively shaped by the past of the
feasibility and inevitability of an international development trust. The specific technical steps that might be
taken to implement the SDT will turn on the total context prevailing at the time. The major impediment will
not be technical, but rather psychological: the SDT will
be implemented amidst reciprocal suspicions of deceitful
intentions. Although the behavior of the parties directly
involved may, by demonstrating manifest intention,
diminish the gnawing fear of betrayal, the most effective
psychological strut will certainly be the degree of commitment to and investment in the SDT by public and
private concerns from the rest of the world. Implementa-

tion and the recruitment of foreign support may be conducted in tandem in such a manner that one accelerates and reinforces the other.

The full range of imaginable contextual constructs cannot be considered here; in view of the rich possibilities for variation, it is unwise to suggest a hard and fast schedule and timetable for implementation. Nevertheless, there may be value in considering some variations on a basic scenario, in order to focus clearly on likely problems and to show the feasibility of the entire plan.

The optimal institutional setting for the early planning stages of the SDT would be a comparatively nonpolitical, technical international organization with extensive experience in development projects, preferably but not necessarily located in the Middle East. The organization that most approximates these features is the International Bank for Reconstruction and Development. The Asian and African Development Banks may be considered as alternatives and certainly should be incorporated in the project at later stages, but the World Bank is most preferable for several reasons. First, it is associated with the United Nations and hence is a prominent international symbol. It has, nonetheless, maintained a sharp political independence of the Security Council and the General Assembly. Thus, while institutional channels for communication and coordination with the political organs of the United Nations are readily available, the manifest profile and actual dynamics of the World Bank are politically discrete. Second, the Bank has had extensive experience in coordinating public and private funding and skill in massive development projects in the Third World. The SDT will involve precisely such operations, though on a scale

heretofore untried. Third, the World Bank has partici-
pated in projects in Israel, Jordan, and the United Arab
Republic and hence can be expected to have extensive
mid-elite and elite contacts with each of the governments.
Such contacts will prove invaluable in the early, often
informal consultations that will be necessary.

In the first phase, the World Bank would establish a
preparatory task force, whose function would be to consider the technical feasibility of a multinational, mixed
public and private development trust, as a technique of
guided and accelerated international social and economic
development. Because of the innovative scale of such a
project, it would require extensive consultations. These
activities would, in a research framework, permit a number of public and private concerns in different states to
take some part in the early investigation and planning and
enable the preparatory task force to gain an increasingly
realistic sense of the details of the project. And as the
project gained in realism, groups anxious to participate
in it would hasten forward. The expectation of success
becomes a self-fulfilling prophecy.

As the planning for the SDT acquired a realistic profile, a process of political negotiation would begin. Negotiation would be the most dramatic operation, but not
necessarily the most important. The first phase of this
sequence would involve what we may call parallel international "sibs." The Soviet Union and the United Arab
Republic would clarify their policies in terms of the projected SDT as the United States and Israel clarified theirs.
Joinder of policy differences would take place in American-Russian contacts rather than direct Israeli-Egyptian
talks. The political discussions would increasingly incor-

porate the technical details emerging from the research of the World Bank's task force.

A crucial moment in the evolution of the SDT would occur when the question of the concession was formally raised. The appropriate moment would, accordingly, have to be chosen with diplomatic finesse. The point to be emphasized is that the goal would not be logical progression, but rather diplomatic success; the implementation of the SDT even before it was formally constituted might well contribute to that success. Insofar as the United Arab Republic manifested a readiness to participate in the SDT but Israel proved reluctant, the concession might be negotiated at a very early stage; thus, a seminal SDT would impose further international pressure on Israel to collaborate. Insofar as the United Arab Republic was recalcitrant, a seminal SDT might begin to function in Israeli-occupied Sinai, while Egypt consulted with its real and increasingly urgent interests. As long as one state collaborated with the SDT, the entire Trust itself would become a lever for its plenary implementation. When both states finally agreed to the concession, the seminal or transitional SDT elite would be replaced by the permanent directors, chosen by all parties participating in the Trust.

The precise timetable for Israeli military withdrawal from Sinai would turn on a variety of factors, not the least of which would be the shared expectation that the SDT would serve the regional neutralizing function for which it had, in part, been created. The SDT could begin to function even while Israeli troops were still encamped in Sinai. Once it was functioning and the level of foreign investment in the SDT was sufficiently high to insure an intense international interest in the Trust's continuation, the process of withdrawal could be initiated. In the first phase of this sequence, Israel would withdraw one kilometer from the Suez Canal, and Egypt would dredge the Canal and reopen it to international traffic. In the second phase, the SDT border police would occupy the evacuated kilometer-wide belt on the east bank of the Canal and subject it to plenary SDT supervision. Thereafter, Israeli and Egyptian forces would not deal with each other directly, but only through the mediation of agencies of the SDT. The subsequent tempo and manner of Israeli troop withdrawal from Sinai would be determined by Israel and the SDT. Since the SDT would be regularly implementing its own development plans, the entire Peninsula would be shedding its character of a military arena at the same time as troops were being withdrawn. The regulated change of environment would tend to ease Israeli tensions.

Numerous changes may be introduced into the basic scenario, and alternative plans of implementation can easily be fashioned within a variety of contextual constructs. It is always wise to defer enthusiasm for any single set of operations aimed at implementation, for the touchstone of any type of planning is that it is the overall goal that is important, and not the instrumental plan for its realization. The primary goal of the SDT remains: the vindication of Egyptian sovereignty over Sinai coupled with the effective and peaceful neutralization of Sinai, to be accomplished in a manner that enriches all the inhabitants of the entire region, allies Great Power opponents in positive collaboration, and promotes the conditions that can transform a system of minimum order into a world order of human dignity.

JORDAN AND THE PALESTINIAN ARABS

THE ONLY GROUP in the contemporary Middle Eastern situation with a legitimate grievance is the Palestinian Arabs. By a complex convergence of circumstances, they have been denied the opportunity for self-determination and for twenty years have lived in the most degraded conditions. Despite constant expressions of verbal sympathy, they have been despised by the other Arab peoples and have learned to despise themselves. If the tactics of Al Fatah and the other *fedayeen* groups represent strategic fantasies, they provide, nonetheless, a highly effective form of group therapy, for they have reawakened the precious and crucial human component of self-respect. An equitable solution to the problem of the Palestinian Arabs is not only an exigent moral demand but also a crucial requirement for increasing stability in the Middle East.

For all the Pan-Arab rhetoric of sympathy for the Palestinians, the Arab states have done little but impede efforts to give genuine succor to the Palestinians and have frequently used the Palestinian cause to further their own aims. The Kingdom of Jordan has done even less than Israel in aiding the creation of a Palestinian state. In Gaza, the Egyptians kept the Palestinians in closed settlements that were scarcely distinguishable from concentration camps and did not allow them free movement in Egypt. It is an irony of the 1967 war that it was Israel that gave Gaza residents their first opportunity in twenty years to leave Gaza and to travel to the West Bank and to Jordan, to mingle with other Arabs and to return to Gaza at will. But the Palestinians have provided a symbol and frequently a cover for destabilizing activities in the area. No improvement can be hoped for without a settlement of their claims.

The Palestinian problem can only be understood in its historical context. Palestine is an area that has traditionally included both the contemporary State of Israel and the Kingdom of Jordan. Under the Ottoman Empire, the area of Jordan had been a dormant part of the *vilayet* of Syria. In 1918, Faisal of the Hashemite tribe of Saudi Arabia formed an Arab kingdom encompassing Syria and Jordan. Faisal's government collapsed under French military pressure in 1920, and the British in Palestine consolidated their control over the area of Jordan, while the French Army took control of Syria. In 1921, Faisal's younger brother, the Emir Abdullah, arrived in Jordan with the intention of invading French Syria and restoring his brother to the throne. Winston Churchill, then Colonial Secretary, bought Abdullah off. He created and offered him the Emirate of Transjordan and a monthly subsidy of £5,000; Abdullah accepted, and Transjordan was born. Throughout the interwar period, the Emirate operated under the supervision of a Mandatory Resident in Amman.

In 1946, with the concurrence of the British, Abdullah made himself King of Transjordan, and the *de jure* independence of the country was recognized; Britain continued to grant large subsidies and in return retained extensive residual rights in the country. The year 1946, then, witnessed the first formal partition of Palestine and, in a very real sense, the first deprivation of a right of political self-determination for the Palestinian Arabs. There is no indication that it even occurred to the British to consult the population of Transjordan about its wishes in regard, first, to the secession of the area from historical Palestine and, second, to government by a monarchical system at whose pinnacle sat a non-Palestinian. The point worth emphasizing is that the existence of Israel is only one factor in the instability of the Kingdom of Jordan. The core of domestic instability in Jordan lies in its foundation as a heterarchy, an artificial Hashemite government divergent from the Palestinian character of the population, a creation of the United Kingdom as an instrument of British diplomacy in the region, a state that cannot exist without enormous subsidies from abroad.

At the end of the World War, Jewish communities in the Diaspora were pressing their governments to fulfill the promise of the Mandate and to provide a home for the displaced remnant of European Jewry. Britain surrendered the matter to a special session of the United Nations General Assembly at the end of November, which provided for partition of the area into a Jewish and an Arab state with an economic union between them.[*] The Arab countries did not accept the plan, and Arab volunteers from neighboring countries began to attack Jewish settlements; the British threw up their hands at the entire affair and accelerated termination of the Mandate. On May 14, 1948, they departed, and the National Council of the local Jewish community, the *Yishuv*, declared the existence of the State of Israel. Shortly thereafter, the

* For the text of the General Assembly's Resolution, see the Appendix, pp. 100ff.

armies of the surrounding Arab countries invaded the new state.

In the war that followed, the Israeli Army was more successful than its adversaries. The United Nations armistice agreements of 1949 found Israel in possession of sections of the Negev, strips of the midlands and the Galilee, and a small strip of the coast, which had not been granted it in the United Nations partition plan. More tragic was the fact that a million of the Arab residents[†] of the original and acquired areas had fled and formed new refugee populations in two of the major areas that had been assigned to the stillborn Palestinian Arab state by the General Assembly: Gaza, adjacent to Egyptian Sinai, and the broad Palestinian heartland, adjacent to the Kingdom of Jordan. Had the Arab population in these areas been independent, it might have formed the Palestinian state envisaged in the General Assembly partition plan and possibly, as the economic union took shape, negotiated return of the areas lost in the war. Unfortunately, these areas were controlled by Egypt and Jordan respectively and were ultimately assimilated (formally in Jordan's case) to their national territories. By this *de facto* if not *de jure* action, a second major group of Palestinian Arabs had been denied the right to self-determination.

A third group of Palestinians remained within the borders of Israel. There has been much lament about their plight, but in material and security terms, they live far above the level of minimum toleration. Yet if one accepts the notion that a crucial element of self-respect in this

[†] On the problem of the number of Palestine refugees, see the "Comment" on pp. 58ff.

era is identification with a nation-state in which one is a "full" citizen, the Arab minority in Israel cannot be happy. Israel was created in order to be a Jewish state, and although there is an internal tension between secular and ethnicist trends, the general complexion of the state in the foreseeable future will remain ethnicist. Even the most cosmopolitan Arab living in these circumstances will undergo some psychic tension as he seeks to accommodate himself to what is, if not a hostile, then at least an alien environment. It should be no surprise that Israeli Arabs have associated themselves with the Palestine national cause; the third major group of Palestinian Arabs has likewise been denied self-determination.

Until June of 1967, there was, in fact, a Palestinian state, including the areas east of the Jordan and the heartland of Palestine, west of the Jordan. Of its 1.8 million inhabitants, about 1.4 million identified themselves as Palestinians. Because of an uncoordinated convergence of Arab and Western policy, this state was not called Palestine, but rather the Hashemite Kingdom of Jordan. Regrettably, the bard's dictum that "a rose by any other name smells just as sweet" has not held true for the Palestinian inhabitant of Jordan. He views himself as a displaced person in a foreign country. And since June of 1967, the Arab areas west of the Jordan have been occupied, and the inhabitants live under the dominion of the enemy.

Two contradictory considerations weigh heavily upon the Big Power negotiators. First, without reference to past responsibilities for their misery, the Arabs of Palestine are entitled to every equity possible in an ultimate solution. Allegations of guilt or responsibility, of "evil for evil," can be laid to rest along with other atavistic criminal law conceptions. There is not and never was any moral reason for "punishing" the Palestinian Arabs, and there is, in any case, no deterrent power in such a course. The plight of the Palestinians has been utterly wretched. If there is to be any effective international succor for these people, it must involve giving them the means to help themselves.

Second, and perhaps paradoxically, the most basic and intense demand of the Palestinian Arabs cannot be assuaged. What the Palestinian Arabs want is the termination of the Israeli state and the creation of an Arab majority state, which would probably include the eastern as well as the western sectors of the Jordan River. Even were the Four Powers to adopt this goal as their own, it is not a goal that can be realized diplomatically. The Palestinian Arab front well appreciates this fact, hence it has chosen warfare as its instrument and has made no effort to seek a meeting with the Israeli government on the diplomatic level. At this moment, it is the practice of guerrilla warfare that contributes largely to internal and interstate instability in the Middle East.

The symbols of the self-determination of peoples run deep in contemporary myth and doctrine. The right of the Palestinian Arabs to self-determination has been recognized by the United Nations since 1947. In the area east of the Jordan River, Palestinian self-determination is an internal Arab matter; the claims of these Palestinians are not territorial, for they are in Arab Palestine. Their claims relate to popular determination of the form of government and to the name of their state. The peculiar benefits that have accrued to the West by overlooking the Palestinian character of Jordan and by failing to acknowledge that the vast majority of its citizens are Palestinian Arabs have ceased. It is now urgent that the real character of the situation be recognized and formally guaranteed. Writers in this country and in Israel have argued that sooner or later the Palestine nationalist movement will topple Hussein, seize Jordan, create a Palestinian state, and thereby solve the Palestine problem. But if Hussein falls, it is extremely doubtful that the highly publicized but quite small Palestine Liberation Army will secure control of Jordan. More likely, Syria, Iraq, and Saudi Arabia, which have long cast covetous eyes on Jordan, will snatch it up or divide it among themselves. Even Israel might shuffle itself into the deal. In any event, the legitimate aspirations of the Palestinians will have no outlet and will continue as a factor of instability, both within the Arab states and on the international level. Western commitment to the Palestinian character of Jordan is neither pro nor contra Hussein; it is simply a deterrent against outsiders intervening in that state. The effectiveness of this deterrent depends on a lucid communication of intention.

The major diplomatic challenge relates to the Arab areas west of the Jordan, which were occupied by Israel in June of 1967 and which are densely populated by Palestinian Arabs. In international law, the status of this latter area is ambiguous. According to the General Assembly of the United Nations, the West Bank was to have been part of a Palestinian Arab state.* But Jordan annexed it unilaterally in 1948, and Israel has occupied it since 1967. The only party having anything approaching a clear international legal title to the area is the inchoate Palestinian

* For the text of the plan, see the Appendix, pp. 100ff.

Arab community, successor to the stillborn Arab Palestine, envisaged and authorized by the United Nations in 1947. The optimum solution would be return of this area to that community. The West Bank could then pursue a number of alternatives. It could form a separate Arab state or associate itself with Jordan or with Israel or with both.

Such a resolution of the problem would have several attractions for Israel. In the most profound if subtle sense, it would stop the corrosive effects of micro-colonialism that will inevitably set in if Israel tries to rule a large alien and hostile population or to create an Arab Bantustan. The Idumean period is one of the least glorious of Jewish history, and it comports poorly with a modern social democracy. Creation of an Arab state would also shift a tremendous moral burden from Israeli shoulders, for if Israel is not the cause of the Palestinian dispersion, circumstances have forced it to be an unwilling accomplice. In one simple and relatively painless operation, Israel could be the major architect of a genuine Palestinian state. The creation of a legitimate Palestinian government would also facilitate the compensation of Arab citizens who lost property in the 1948 and 1967 periods, which may diminish some of the acrimony; hitherto, Palestinian claims have been aired by other Arab governments for their own political purposes and with scant evidence of any real concern for actual payment or for the plight of the Palestinians.

Nor would this solution pose a security hazard to Israel. Insecurity in the Jordan River area stems from Palestinian commando activity, which would in part be obviated and in part deflected by the creation of a Palestinian state.

Even if commando activity continued, Israel would find it considerably easier to engage in effective and legitimate response. Until now, Israel's retaliations to such actions have been inhibited by the absence of a legitimate target; Hussein has made it clear that he would like to restrain the Palestinian militants but is unable to do so. Paradoxically, each Israeli response weakens Hussein and increases the prestige and power of the militant Palestinian movement. The existence of a Palestinian state from which attacks originated would provide a legitimate target and would render the threat of Israeli retaliations an effective deterrent to aggression and terrorism.

Despite incessant reiteration of the necessity for the agreement of all Arab states to a resolution of the Middle Eastern situation, the fact is that the West Bank solution requires only Israeli and United Nations action. Israel need only announce that it will withdraw from the West Bank regions occupied in 1967 upon formation of a representative Palestinian government recognized as independent and sovereign by the United Nations and committed to active compliance with the principles and purposes of the United Nations Charter. Israel would then permit the United Nations Committee on Non-Self-Governing Territories to dispatch an observer team to the West Bank, which would administer a series of referenda: the inhabitants would determine the form of government they wished and would choose their political leaders. Israel would thereafter withdraw under a United Nations timetable. The United Nations might station a peace-keeping force on the eastern and western boundaries of the new Palestinian state, but this would be a largely symbolic gesture. Israel would have scant interest in reentering, and Hussein's interest in reannexation would be tempered by the realization that he would thereby lose Western support and jeopardize his precarious hold on his own throne by stirring the Palestinian majority within his own country to rise against him. Hussein has in fact declared that he will facilitate Palestinian self-determination on the West Bank.

Uhuru is an overture and not a finale; internal developments within the nascent Palestinian state cannot be predicted. But many fears that are now expressed seem quite exaggerated. The fear that no Palestinian leader of any stature will commit himself to a compromise or partial solution is unfounded. Vacuums in politics are, unfortunately, short-lived. Palestinian leaders may hedge by characterizing a West Bank regime as "temporary" or "provisional," but someone will step forward. Because nothing is more permanent than the provisional, the most effective Palestinian leaders may well draft themselves or use proxies. Palestine will not be leaderless. It is more likely that it will suffer from a surfeit of leaders and civil violence may ensue. If this were a disqualification from statehood, the membership of the United Nations would be rapidly depleted. Personal power struggles are no monopoly of the Middle East, and equivalents of the contending ideologies there can be found throughout the world. This is a mark of our times. No one can say at what point Palestinians (or others) will insist that power struggles be limited to an internal political rather than military arena. This is obviously a matter for the Palestinians themselves to decide.

Modes of Implementation

The Palestinian state could be established under certain negotiated conditions, which might guarantee or enhance the security of all surrounding states. One need not, at this time, spell out or speculate on the content of these conditions. But it is worth emphasizing that there are precedents in contemporary international law for the joint establishment, by adversaries, of a state contiguous to both, which is subject to conditions aimed at preventing the new state from becoming noxious to either of its progenitors. Postwar Austria is a rough but by no means irrelevant model.

Israel is the pivotal participant in this solution, as it well appreciates, and the intense public discussion of "the recognition of a Palestine entity" indicates that Israelis have been considering a possibility of this type. But if the intemperate statements of the Minister of Information, Israel Galili, reflect the thinking of the government, Israel is quite unprepared psychologically for such a step. In a rancorous exchange of public letters with Professor Jacob Talmon,* Galili stated that he did not believe that the Palestinian Arabs exhibited the consciousness of a political entity, that they had not produced national leaders, and that the people themselves had shown no desire to form a separate political state. This is almost traditionally wishful; the facts of Palestine nationalism are both grim and eloquent. To ignore them is to invite their inten-

* J. Talmon, "An Open Letter to the Minister Israel Galili," *Ma'ariv* (May 16, 1969), p. 12; I. Galili, "An Answer to Professor Jacob Talmon," *Ma'ariv* (May 22, 1969), p. 12. Galili was not, he said, speaking for the government, but he seems to have expressed the sense of the political elite.

sification and the degeneration of Israel into a police state.

Israel is built on a Jewish history of trauma and of personal and group insecurity. The anguish of the Nazi holocaust is a vivid factor in Israeli thinking; Shukairy-type rhetoric, which has survived Ahmed Shukairy's eclipse as *soi-disant* leader of the Palestinians, makes it difficult not to think in defensive and almost paranoiac terms. In this context, the doctrine of "expand or perish" has a superficial plausibility, and there seems to be an almost inexorable logic of survival in retaining the West Bank and Gaza at all costs. But in both immediate and long-range terms, the purported advantages of holding these areas are fantasies. In 1793, Jeremy Bentham said "Emancipate Your Colonies"

> because you have no right to govern them, because they had rather not be governed by you, because it is against their interest to be governed by you, because you get nothing by governing them, because you cannot keep them, because the expense of trying to keep them would be ruinous, because your constitution would suffer by your keeping them, because your principles forbid you to keep them, and because you would do good to all the world by parting with them.

The West did not heed Bentham's advice, and many of its current crises, including perhaps the xenophobia of the Middle East, can be traced to this error. Israel cannot afford to make the same mistake. Unless Israel has the courage to recognize the demands of the Palestinians and shows enough political maturity to deal with men who have terrorized them (as the British did with the Israelis two decades ago, when Stern was the Habash and Lechi was the Fatah of the Middle East), a surging source of instability will continue. Galili is a conscientious civil servant and is dedicated to the security of his state. But he and those who side with him must realize that military and geographical factors are only one part of national security.

The territory seized in the dramatic military successes of 1967 has created an anguishing dilemma for Israelis. The post-1967 "Land of Israel Movement" clearly sees itself as the agent and forerunner of the Holy Jewish Empire, but this is not an entirely new phenomenon. There have always been opposition groups—secular and clerical—that preached expansion on political and security as well as mystical religious grounds. And, in a sense, the territorial metaphysics of the Jewish State have never been thoroughly clarified. The acceptance of the majority UNSCOP plan* represented an unequivocal commitment to specific territorial boundaries and coexistence with a Palestinian Arab state. Subsequent official public assurances of no expansionist ambitions have reinforced this position, as did Israeli withdrawal from Sinai after the first Suez war.

The deep personal and national insecurity engendered by protracted crisis frequently suspends rational thinking aimed at crisis abatement and replaces it with compulsive quantitative responses: more ships, more bombs, more offensive defense, more territory for a defensive buffer. But security is more complex than an artifacted arithmetical reality; the multiplication of seemingly basic instruments of defense may often *decrease* rather than increase national security. The United States is in the

* See the Appendix, pp. 100ff.

process of learning that more missiles do not mean greater security and, paradoxically, that arithmetical responses, in the contemporary world, actually decrease national security. Israelis might well ponder this lesson.

The exacerbated insecurity of the period following the war in 1967 has strengthened the hands of the expansionists in Israel considerably. Security is not always enhanced by control of more territory; increased defense expenditures, extended compulsory military service, the growing number of Israelis killed and wounded on the borders, and the ineluctable attenuation of civil liberty in a period of crisis arouse serious doubts about the advisability of extra-territorial control in this case. Nor has the control of territory improved a defensive posture. The Israeli proponent of territorial retention, like his American counterpart, the proponent of ABM, is motivated by an imperative of territorial defense that contemporary weapons have long since obsolesced. Flying and missile time between Tel Aviv and Amman is the same no matter who controls the West Bank of the Jordan. Israeli control of Sinai does not change the missile distance between Cairo and Tel Aviv. No matter how much territory it controls, *any* state on the Mediterranean is open from the sea to quick attack by aircraft flying below the radar threshold. This is not to suggest that territory has no strategic importance. The strategic value of territory is a function of a broad, multifaceted context; in many circumstances, territory is not of major importance.

Security is always relative, and in the Middle East it will continue to be comparatively fluid as long as there is intense enmity between the peoples of the region. If control of a particular piece of territory increases hostilities, it lowers rather than raises the security position of the occupier. Maximum security in the region is acquired by lowering the overall hostility level. A Palestinian Arab state on the West Bank may not seal Israel's eastern border, but it may well pacify it increasingly over time, insofar as the demands of one belligerent group in the region are satisfied. Is it not significant that Israeli withdrawal from Sinai in 1956 purchased a decade of nonviolence on the Egyptian-Israeli border?

A Comment on the "Numbers Game": Who is a Palestine Refugee?

The reader will have noted my unwillingness even to approach specificity in estimating the number of Palestine refugees. Different numbers and competing formulas have been put forward: from several hundred thousand to more than a million and a half. The divergences are less a matter of gross error than of different premises in a different ethical calculus. These competing numbers become components of political programs that call for radically different courses of compensation and rehabilitation.

Designation of individuals as members of a group should be executed in order to secure certain preferred political outcomes; at the very least, the probable political consequences of alternate designations should be carefully considered. If one is concerned with designing a regional social system of minimum order (not to speak, for the moment, of a system of social justice), an aggregate of crucial importance is comprised of those whose sense of deprivation is so great that they can envision movement toward a tolerable existence only in violent radical change. By "Palestine refugees," I refer broadly to that group of individuals in the Palestine area whose lives have been disrupted by political changes since 1947 to such an extent that they can be returned to a level of self-satisfying productivity and social integration only through massive planning and external aid. This definition is not open-ended; it is bound on the one hand by political goals and on the

[58]

other by the exigencies of the context. It obviously requires a good deal of investigation and thought before it can be applied.

Competing definitions do not fill the minimum-order needs of the Middle East. The statistical approach to the number of Palestine refugees assembles the details of group membership at a certain moment in time—for example, 1949-1950—and continues to define a refugee as either the original statistic or the heir to his identity card. It overlooks aggregates such as Arabs within Israel whose national and material aspirations are unfulfilled, while it may continue to include Palestinian families that have long since settled elsewhere. It makes no distinction between levels of need of different Palestinians. Another statistical approach chooses certain "cut-off" dates after which Arabs who settled in Palestine are not to be considered Palestine refugees even though they were displaced by the events of the late 1940's and have not yet successfully resettled. They remain displaced "Syrians," "Jordanians," and so on. This is the obverse of the "cut-off" date that certain Palestinian militants wish to apply to Jews who will be permitted to remain after "Liberation." It is just as specious, for chronological time is a triviality. Social time and, in particular, cultural identifications are crucial in dealing with the aspirations of human beings.

Charitable groups that have been concerned with ameliorating the conditions of refugees tend to enumerate refugees in terms of their own or similar programs. Those to whom they can or wish to give succor are refugees. This sort of circular definition has high esthetic value in law, where it becomes an instrument of self-legitimization, but it palpably fails to come to grips with the real human problems of the Middle East. It defines goals and the limits of political action in terms of what is being done. But there is no reason why a bad situation should be institutionalized.

Another approach to the numbers problem incorporates the legal criteria of a claimant with sufficient "standing" to lodge his claim before a hypothetical tribunal. This criterion tends to minimize the number of refugees, for laws of property in both the West and Middle East crystallized when the economic class that happened to be ascendant conceived of wealth in certain restricted categories. Nonpropertied classes whose wealth or status consisted in an intricate network of social collaborations—on the street, in the village, in the family or clan, and so on—are excluded, by definition, even though they suffered equally severe losses and even though their continuing deprivation constitutes a destabilizing factor in the

Middle East. The claimant approach is also inadequate because it incorporates by implication sets of social relationships that have since been obsolesced. Consider the case of a family of twenty individuals, spread over three or four generations, who lived on their farm in the Galilee. They fled in 1948. Their claim to a collective patrimony can return them to a status of self-sufficiency only if they return to the original setting. But after ten or fifteen years in a refugee town, their pattern of social relationships will have decisively changed. They cannot be returned to the previous system, and compensation, in its terms, will be woefully inadequate for rehabilitation.

One other difficulty with the claimant criterion is that it involves local laws that were not created for and do not fit the policy needs of the current situation. The automatic application of these laws has limited even further the Palestinian claimants. For example, under Ottoman Turkish land law, still in force in Israel, one category of land escheats to the government when it is abandoned. Arabs who owned this type of land cannot be legal claimants in the strict sense of the term. They are obviously political claimants and should be recognized as such on the international level.

The "numbers game" can be used to minimize one's own responsibility for others or, alternately, to magnify the responsibility of one's adversary. It is thus not surprising that Israelis have tended to shrink the number of refugees and Arabs have tended to bloat it. Both of these approaches conceal a continuation of the conflict by shifting the battle to the question of who is responsible. But linking responsibility and the human needs for compensation and rehabilitation is simply changing compensation into a new form of punitive sanction. There is no such link! From a practical standpoint, the rehabilitation of the displaced and disrupted populations of the Middle East will require an international effort, with a very careful blending of resource and symbolic components. The "Palestine refugees" must be used as a functional term for those in the area of conflict whose needs must be satisfied in order to establish a system of regional order.

· I V ·

SYRIA AND GOLAN

P RESIDENT NASSER has been frantically prodigal in iden-
tifying scapegoats for the Arab debacle he initiated in
1967. After pillorying the United States and exhausting
the local supply, he turned his attention to Syria. Nasser,
ultimately responsible for the war, deserves no exonera-
tion, yet Syria's catalytic role must be recognized. Syrian
gun emplacements in the Golan Heights were firing regularly and accurately upon Israeli settlements throughout
April and May of 1967, guerrillas were trained and dis-
patched, and Radio Damascus was persistently exhorting
the Arab world to "liberate" Palestine. Syrian taunts may
well have helped Nasser fall over the brink he himself
created. Most important, the Syrian stance of extreme
Arab militancy continues unabated. Syria is the center of
commando training, it has remained aloof from the Jarring missions, and it has been uncompromising in its
demands for the destruction of Israel. The average Israeli
citizen probably feels more rancor toward Syria than
toward any other of its enemies. And, indeed, the successive governments in Damascus have been irresponsible in
the extreme, pursuing fantastic and disastrous foreign and
domestic policies and sporting eye-patches as to probable
consequences. If the succession of Syrian political elites
has innovated anything, it is the institutionalization of
instability.

The prospects for some degree of political stability
within Syria and, hence, of more rational external behavior are poor. The Syrian population is extremely hetero-

geneous, and the political process is carried on by a number of intensely conflicting sects and ethnic groups. The symbols of Ba'ath and Arab socialism frequently disguise only personal and ethnic struggles for power. Syrian political groups have been unable to establish enough of a common ground to pursue a joint and stable program of government and development. The exception, of course, is hostility to Israel, and the rival groups have tried to outdo each other in this unproductive field. A ruling elite requires a legitimating myth. Where the elite can provide no palpable service to the people it controls, it will frequently resort to a fantasied Manichean struggle to justify the continued exercise of power. Numerous revolutions throughout the Third World that have proved to be barren of positive social results now justify themselves as opponents of "neo-imperialism" and "neo-colonialism," even as heroic leaders themselves concoct the conspiracies they will uncover and exorcise. In the Middle East, Zionism is often invoked as a variant synonym of cosmic evil. Without such a scapegoat, no Syrian regime could possibly justify its claim to power.

The occupation of the Syrian Golan Heights in 1967 was deferred until Egyptian forces had been decisively shattered on the Sinai front. Thereafter, the Israelis stormed the Syrian gun emplacements with singleminded intensity and secured the area at tremendous cost. The Israeli determination to silence the artillery that had been firing with impunity on the settlements below is indicative of a deeply embedded Israeli attitude.

The great human problems encountered on the West Bank do not arise in Golan. The Heights were sparsely populated, and a comparatively small group of Syrians has been dispossessed by the Israeli occupation. The Four Power negotiations could conceivably ignore the Syrian front, much as the Syrians have ignored the Jarring mission, but this approach would leave an exposed flank on which further trouble could fester. On the other hand, a simple legitimization of Israeli occupation would assure future Syrian governments of regular demagogic ammunition. Far graver is the certainty that it would colonialize Israel, a corrosive trend both internally and externally. Explicit consideration must be given to the problem of Golan.

Ironically, it is the large number of Druze in the Golan area who may provide the beginning of a solution. One must note, as a most general observation, that the frequent characterization of participants in the Middle East drama as "Arabs and Jews" is a gross oversimplification of an extremely complex and heterogeneous regional population. Although it is useful for proponents of Pan-Arabism to speak of the drive for union shared by all the Arab peoples of the area, the fact is that the Middle East is an ethnic, racial, and religious patchwork, of which the Arabs are only one part. And the Arabs themselves are split by sect and tribal divisions, often expressing themselves in intense hostility and periodic violence. On close investigation, the "Pan-Arab" is about as elusive as the "Czechoslovak"; Pan-Arabism and even Arabism often prove to be nothing more than the ambitions of particular political elites.

The role of ethnic or tribal identifications in international politics is only now gaining our full appreciation. The longer-range implications are obvious. The intensity of ethnic identifications is increasing both because of their

[63]

own dynamics and because of the exclusivity of other ethnic groups. In areas of the world only now undergoing politicization, traditional ethnic identifications are providing a much more compelling focus for political loyalties than are the symbols of the "nation-state." Where political boundaries had been drawn without regard to ethnic identifications, politicization of the masses has set off, not a process of unification, but rather a process of fractionation. (This is a phenomenon hardly limited to the Third World.) The lesson is clear. The establishment of effective political units about the globe must take account of the persistence of ethnic identifications. Supraethnic structures have relatively little chance of enduring in highly ethnicized environments. (The obverse corollary has, alas, been equally apparent: a quick way of destabilizing an established nation-state is to find the ethnic fissures and to probe them.)

The Middle East is an object lesson in the power of ethnic loyalties to reinforce or wrench apart political structures. The establishment of Arab nations after Turkish defeat in the First World War was a tribal rather than national rank-and-file phenomenon. The states that have proved most viable have been either ethnically cohesive (for example, Israel) or institutionally balanced with full recognition of ethnic divisions (for example, Lebanon).*

---

* Each of these examples, in turn, emphasizes the instability of institutionalized ethnic balances. The Lebanese balance is based on an old census, which has been made obsolescent by major demographic changes. But Lebanese elites and external powers continue to find it convenient to mythologize the census. At least one crisis per decade points up the volatility of Lebanon and the extremely modest administrative ambitions of the official Lebanese government. In Israel, in contrast, socioeconomic differences are perceived

The states that have shown themselves to be least viable have been the most ethnically mixed. The fifty-year struggle of the Kurds in Iraq may be only a harbinger of numerous national movements dotting the entire Middle East. And current solutions that seek any degree of effectiveness must take the ethnic factor fully into account.

These considerations have direct relevance to the problem of the optimum disposition of Golan. Druze predominate in the region. The Druze are members of a fiercely independent religious sect, who claim descent from Jethro, the father-in-law of Moses. Because they were zealous and rather secretive in the practice of their religion, and perhaps because they viewed themselves as racially different, they were traditionally ill-treated by Arabs in some areas. In the 1948 Arab-Israeli war, the Palestinian Druze community numbering some 25,000 joined the Israelis, and since the war, the Druze have enjoyed full citizenship, even serving in the Army. The primary community demand that the Druze have made on Israel has been for religious autonomy; the Israelis have granted this, as they do to all religious communities, in accordance with the constitutional structure of the state.

If our era is indeed characterized by the demand for political self-determination of discrete groups, then it is predictable that the Druze, at some point in the future, will begin to make such a claim. It may be accelerated by

---

in terms of ethnic origin; there is an apparent tension between those who view themselves as "Europeans" and those who view themselves as "Orientals." The presence of ethnic divisions does not, of course, lead inevitably to overt conflict. Countertrends of homogenization are operating and can be accelerated by an elite holding the reins of the communications network—assuming, naturally, that the elite is so disposed.

the growing number of Druze who study in Israeli universities and hence are directly exposed to contemporary doctrines of nationalism and self-determination. When these young Druze do begin to articulate their demands, tension will be generated, not only in Israel but in Syria and Lebanon as well. For the Druze are an irredentist people, and more than 100,000 of them live across the border in Syria and almost 90,000 in Lebanon.

The Big Power negotiators might well consider the possibility of urging Israel to declare the Golan Heights a trust territory for the Druze under Chapters XI and XII of the United Nations Charter. The institution of international trusteeship, a carry-over from the mandate system of the League of Nations, was primarily aimed at the internationally supervised development of mandate territories and colonies leading to their independence. Yet neither the language of the United Nations Charter nor the policy it expresses militates against application of the international doctrine of trusteeship to contemporary situations caused by changes in political boundaries. Article 73 of the Charter provides:

Members of the United Nations which have or assume responsibilities for the administration of territories whose peoples have not yet attained a full measure of self-government recognize the principle that the interests of the inhabitants of these territories are paramount and accept as a sacred trust the obligation to promote to the utmost, within the system of international peace and security established by the present Charter, the well-being of the inhabitants of these territories, and, to this end:

[66]

a. to ensure, with due respect for the culture of the peoples concerned, their political, economic, social, and educational advancement, their just treatment, and their protection against abuses;

b. to develop self-government, to take due account of the political aspirations of the peoples, and to assist them in the progressive development of their free political institutions, according to the particular circumstances of each territory and its peoples and their varying stages of advancement;

c. to further international peace and security;

d. to promote constructive measures of development, to encourage research, and to cooperate with one another and, when and where appropriate, with specialized international bodies with a view to the practical achievement of the social, economic, and scientific purposes set forth in this Article; and

e. to transmit regularly to the Secretary-General for information purposes, subject to such limitation as security and constitutional considerations may require, statistical and other information of a technical nature relating to economic, social, and educational conditions in the territories for which they are respectively responsible other than those territories to which Chapters XII and XIII apply.

The phrase "members . . . which have or assume responsibilities for the administration of territories whose peoples have not yet attained a full measure of self-government" would appear to include a state such as Israel and a territory such as Golan, for Article 73 does not discuss formal international legal rights but only the question of responsibility for administration. Indeed, Article 77 reiterates that trusteeship may apply to "territories voluntarily placed under the system by states responsible for their administration." Nor would the word "territories" exclude Golan, whereas the word "state" might have done so. In fact, the basic principle of Chapters XI and XII of the Charter is that the inhabitants of a region are the fundamental "sovereigns." If the General Assembly accepted Israel's trust declaration and a trusteeship agreement were negotiated, the United Nations would acquire a degree of supervision over the Golan area with the assurance that its development would proceed in conformity with international law; in return, Israel would acquire a seat on the Trusteeship Council, under Article 86. And the international legal precedent of no acquisition of territory by military means would be vindicated.

Recognition by the General Assembly and by the Trusteeship Council of an Israeli trust over the Druze national home would have a number of consequences. First, the area would be politically neutralized, and ultimately a buffer state would be created between Israel and Syria. Second, until this state emerged, Israel would exercise *trust* and not *sovereign* responsibilities over the area, policing its outermost border, not for Israeli but for Druze occupation. This approach would obviate Israeli imperialist expansion and yet prevent Syria from returning to the crucial Golan Heights and threatening Israeli settlements below. Third, the anticipation of a Druze state would minimize the national and transnational tensions involved in eventual Druze claims for self-determination and permit young Druze activists to channel their energies into creative nation-building rather than violent and frequently destructive protest. Finally, the long record of Druze-Israeli trust and cooperation would assure the Druze community of protection by the ideal international trustee until stable institutions of statehood had been created. A Druze state might ultimately become part of an economic union including both Israel and adjoining Arab states, perhaps catalyzing broader regional federation.

Any social situation is complex, and no solution ever involves application of only a single policy. A lawful decision taken by the international community to support the territorial self-determination of a particular ethnic, linguistic, or religious group involves consideration of many extant and projected factors. In addition to such obvious considerations as the viability of the proposed state and the older entity and the security impact on surrounding states, one must recognize that self-determination acquires grave significance since it defers some of the most comprehensive human-rights policies by creating a group of exclusive identification. But even when self-determination looms as the best of alternatives, it is well to remember that no decision is final. Patterns of social and economic interaction and political organization change. With all due deference to Hegel, the state is not a natural phenomenon; it is a cultural creation, and over time it may be absorbed in functional communities of more inclusive identification. An appreciation of the panorama of possibilities offered by a broader temporal perspective may show that, in certain contexts, a tentative move toward the political self-determination of a particular group may, by increasing regional order, maximize the potential for more inclusive forms of political integration in the future.

Ideally, the creation of a Druze Trust Territory should involve both Israel and the Arab states. Yet, assuming Syrian abstention and even denunciation, the Trust can be created solely by Israel and the United Nations. The first step, of course, must be Israel's: a unilateral declaration of intention. Nothing is hazarded by such a declaration; should it be rejected by the United Nations General Assembly, the current status of effective control would continue.

V

JERUSALEM

THE UNITED NATIONS partition plan of 1947 had sought to resolve the conflicting claims to Jerusalem by creating an international status for the city. The plan never came to fruition. During the 1948 war, the Old City of Jerusalem was occupied by the Arab Legion, and after the armistice, it was annexed by Jordan. Although the Jordanian government promised to fulfill the international guarantees of access for all faiths, the Jews were excluded from Jerusalem from 1948 to 1967, and several Jewish holy places, whose sanctity was guaranteed under the United Nations plan, were desecrated. At the same time, the Israelis nationalized their sector of Jerusalem. In June of 1967, the Israelis occupied the West Bank, and although they have continued to treat that area as occupied territory, they have, in effect, annexed the Old City of Jerusalem. Given the intense religious and political significance that Judaism attaches to Jerusalem, no Israeli politician can seriously recommend surrender of the city without terminating his own career. From the Israeli standpoint, Jerusalem is the least negotiable item on the agenda—if the issue of negotiation is withdrawal.

Internationalization of the city as planned in 1947 still holds a number of attractions. First, it would tend to neutralize the controversial political status of Jerusalem. Second, it would provide relatively firm guarantees of access to holy places by all the faiths concerned. Third, it would involve the international community in continuous supervision of one crucial border in the area. Yet the problems of internationalization are enormous. Israel has little faith in the United Nations; a significant segment of the General Assembly membership has aligned itself with the Arab cause for ideological as well as short-range political reasons. From the Israeli standpoint, internationalization might be the first step toward return of Jerusalem to Arab control and an indefinite exclusion of Jews from the city. Furthermore, given the present polarization of the global arena, internationalization might simply transform a regional problem into an international problem with higher antes and potentially more dreadful payoffs.

Internationalization, it should be emphasized, is a policy and not a program. The realization of the policy may involve a wide variety of programs, from supervision by any of a number of international organizations, each having a different decision structure, to national control under formal international guarantees. In the latter sense, Jerusalem was internationalized from 1948 to 1967 in that the Kingdom of Jordan exercised suzerainty under specific and verbally accepted international stipulations regarding access to the holy places of the faiths. In point of fact, the Jordanian government did not discharge its international responsibilities as keeper of the holy places. Thus, two decades of experience support the proposition that some blend of internationalization and sovereign control is a precedent, but that the Jordanian government has demonstrated that it does not have the capacity to acquit itself of the obligations attached to this mixed national and international role. The diplomatic challenge is the invention of a form of internationalization that can best accommodate the interests of all the religious and political groups concerned with Jerusalem.

Jerusalem is a unique cultural and political phenomenon because of its religious significance to Judaism, Islam, and all the Christian sects. Although spiritual and emotional involvements have almost equalized the different religious concerns with the city, it is useful to note the variations in doctrinal significance attached to Jerusalem by the different faiths. For the Moslem, Jerusalem is one among a number of holy cities, the most important being Mecca (a pilgrimage or *haj* to which is a crucial sacrament). Jerusalem does not have a singular political significance in Islamic theocratic doctrines. For the Christian, pilgrimage to Jerusalem and the other holy places has been a traditional practice; a number of sects invest in the act an importance comparable to the Islamic *haj*. But since the Middle Ages, the question of political control of Jerusalem has not been a major Christian concern. For the Jew, however, Jerusalem is the exclusive theocratic city. A thrice-annual pilgrimage to the city is a sacrament, burial in or near the city facilitates integral resurrection, and, most important, the rebirth of the Jewish Commonwealth, a unique blend of political and religious messianism, is inextricably tied to the rebuilding of the sacred capital. In short, from the standpoint of religio-political doctrines, Islam and Christianity require unimpeded access to and protection of the holy places; Judaism, imparting as it does a sacramental character to the city, requires its political control as the capital of the Jewish Commonwealth. Hence, were a contemporary statesman free to fashion an ideal religio-political status for Jerusalem, accommodating the most intense demands of the three major religions concerned with it, he would probably accord a nominal sovereignty to the Jews and incorporate effective and enforceable guarantees of autonomy and unimpeded access by adherents of the other faiths to their respective holy places. He would, in fact, articulate the essential model followed from 1948 to 1967, with one major difference: Israel rather than Jordan would be the international keeper of the holy places. This change would stem both from Jordan's record of failure in fulfilling the international obligations of free access and from Israel's unique need for symbolic control of Jerusalem.

Two decades of Jordanian experience in Jerusalem have demonstrated that a unilateral declaration on the international level promising to fulfill international obligations is not a sufficient political or psychological guarantee of compliance. It is rather unfair to judge Israeli capacity to play the role of impartial custodian on the basis of only two years of practice; in the past year, in particular, serious security problems in the Old City have complicated Israel's task enormously. But it is clear that in the current political context, and even with the best intentions, neither a Jewish nor an Arab state can fulfill the requirements of custodianship without some system of international supervision. Judaism is not an ecumenical faith, and many Jewish religious leaders harbor deep suspicions and hostilities toward other religions. It is not difficult to imagine individual Christians being barred from the country and, hence, from Jerusalem because of asserted missionary intentions, nor is it difficult to foresee Moslem leaders being barred from the country either because of their political intentions or the unintended political consequences of their presence. Beyond the individual injustice of these cases, the broader political ramifications cannot be gauged. And the mundane municipal functions in the Old City are susceptible to a variety of interpretations and colorations. Whether or not Israeli acts are really aimed at reducing the Arab population or dislodging them from profitable commercial locations or are legitimate exercises of eminent domain for purposes of slum clearance and urban renewal, each exercise of political power has excited fierce responses among Jerusalem Arabs as well as among the Arabs of the neighboring states. Some form of internationalization is necessary to supervise municipal decisions and to shift the full onus from Israeli shoulders.

Some options are not available. Prominent Israeli diplomats have indicated that although Israel will not withdraw from the city, it will concede Jordanian authority over Moslem shrines and permit the Jordanian flag to be flown over them. Even assuming that Jordan does have a legitimate claim to the city (a claim that the United States has never recognized and that Palestinian assertions may supersede), unified Jerusalem is much more than an urban shrine. It is a city in which a sizeable non-Jewish, non-Israeli population lives. National and juridical protection is not vouchsafed for these groups by the proposed Israeli concession. That Israel is an ethnic state makes it exceedingly injudicious to permit an alien group to come involuntarily under its exclusive jurisdiction.

Former Ambassador Lewis Jones has suggested appointment of an international religious trust over the holy places, which would provide not only for their governance but also for their improvement. But this approach would solve only part of the problem. Many of the holy places are not severable from the life of the city and are not divisible among competing sects, for the convergence of religious loyalties does not attach only to the city as a whole but also to many of the specific shrines within it. The Dome of the Rock, for example, holy to Islam, stands over part of the ancient Temple area, which is sacrosanct to Jews. Thus, a system of dividing sovereignty within the city for the shrines of each sect is not practicable. Yet in the current political context, leaving such ecumenical holy places in the exclusive jurisdiction of Israel is extremely dangerous. Rebuilding the Temple in the twentieth century seems somewhat fantastic, but Palestine is an extraordinary place, characterized by extreme contrasts of ruthless modernism and atavistic traditionalism; and the rebirth of a Jewish Commonwealth itself is hardly less than fantastic. If this scenario of a Temple reconstruction, launched by domestic clerical parties and foreign religious groups, seems far-fetched, archeological excavations infringing Islamic shrines are not. Nor is it difficult to imagine Jewish terrorist destruction of the Dome in the midst of a regional crisis, as a way of ending "once and for all" Islamic concern with the city. There is, already, one example of such Christian extremism.

The volatility of Jerusalem as an immediate and future political problem cannot be overstated. The danger of even the mildest Israeli infringements on Islamic shrines can escalate the current crisis and create a genuine and unending religious war between Jew and Moslem with implications extending far beyond the Middle East. Hence, an international regime for Jerusalem must accommodate the integrated nature of many of the holy places with some form of integrated international control that is, at the same time, realizable in the present political circumstances.

A basic challenge to the Four Power negotiators will be the formulation of an international statute for Jerusalem that will be accepted and recognized by the United Nations. Participation in the drafting of this statute should include, in addition to the Four Power negotiators, representatives of Israel, Jordan, the Palestinian Arabs, and the diverse religious groups concerned. But Israel is the only crucial party to this operation, since it exercises effective control in Jerusalem. Any of the other parties could, of course, abstain, but this would only be a self-imposed sanction; the result would not be termination of the drafting but only deprivation of their own opportunity to influence the ultimate form of the administration of Jerusalem.

The Jerusalem Statute would concern municipal government within the city and would attempt to integrate the different religious and ethnic groups in an effective decision structure. It would incorporate substantive provisions guaranteeing the rights of the faiths, unimpeded pilgrimage privileges subject only to conventional health measures, and procedural forms for resolving municipal disputes and responding legislatively to new problems. The optimum procedural form would probably be a joint mayoral and bicameral council system. The mayor would be chosen by popular election of the inhabitants of Jerusalem and would serve as the executive of the city. One house of the City Council—for convenience, let us call it the Curia—would consist of representatives appointed by all the religious sects in the city; its writ would run to legislation in regard to the holy places, but its consent would also be required for those secular decisions made by the second house—let us refer to it as the Senate—affecting religious places or practices. The Senate would be elected popularly on a proportional representation system, insuring representation of each ethnic and religious group in Jerusalem, so long as Jerusalemites chose to identify themselves on ethnic rather than on class or interest lines. The Senate would have jurisdiction over the mundane secular matters of any urban administration.

The Statute would also create a Jerusalem Administrative Tribunal, which would serve as a constitutional court for disputes regarding the interpretation and application of the Statute. Appeal from its judgments would lie to the International Court of Justice through request for an advisory opinion, which would be transmitted to the Economic and Social Council of the United Nations and then submitted to the Court in that organ's name. The International Court's decision would be binding on the Jerusalem and Israeli governments.

There is a semantic abuse committed in speaking of a "binding advisory opinion," but this is an effective legal fiction that has been used elsewhere when parties to an international agreement have sought to employ the International Court as a final international instance of dispute resolution. And if the procedure for referring an appeal to the Court in The Hague seems complex, it is relatively easy to institutionalize and would probably take considerably less time than would docketing and hearing by the Supreme Court of Israel. The advantage of incorporating the International Court in the decision structure of Jerusalem is that protection of the diverse interests of the city by an impartial international guardian would be thereby guaranteed.

The Jerusalem Statute would be negotiated and drafted by an international conference of the religious and secular groups necessarily concerned with aspects of the city. The conference could be convened by Israel and could begin its deliberations even before any of the other area problems were tackled. The ensuing statute for Jerusalem could be adopted by the Israeli government and underwritten by the Four Powers through an exchange of notes. Arab pressure might prevent the United Nations from making it the subject of a resolution, but the Security Council or General Assembly could "take note of it."

Jerusalem would, then, be an Israeli city, operating under a unique statutory system aimed at achieving maximum responsiveness to the needs and desires of an idiosyncratically mixed population. The requirements of the major faiths would be accommodated, and the interests of the inhabitants would be substantively and procedurally secured in a democratic system, with international guarantees.

VI

FROM MINIMUM ORDER TO PEACE

Nous ne coalisons pas les états,
nous unissons des hommes.
JEAN MONNET

THE SOLUTION of every problem requires time, and some problems can be solved only with the passage of time. The vigor and virulence of the deep divisions and enmities that crisscross the Middle East should not be minimized, and it would be naive to believe that they can be magically healed by some form of diplomatic settlement. Time is needed. The optimum focus for diplomatic endeavor is not a quixotic quest for peace in this region, but a search, within the realm of the possible, for a system of minimum order, which can lower the level of overt violence and serve as the groundwork for a future peace. Minimum order may indeed be policed. But, in the final analysis, peace cannot be imposed. It must come from the inhabitants of the region themselves.

The enmity between Arab and Jew is, as we have seen, only one strand in the complex web of the region. Yet it is the most urgent and critical because, if stretched or broken, the entire fabric of Middle Eastern and perhaps global order may disintegrate. Any attempt to construe Israeli behavior as a coeval contribution to regional tension arouses great indignation; the Israelis devoutly believe that they are doing no more than asserting their right to exist. They did not start the war of 1967, and if their genuine effort at self-defense was unprecedentedly successful, they cannot be blamed for the gross incompetence of the would-be aggressors.

The harsh fact is that the June war did not start in May of 1967 or, for that matter, in May of 1948. Its roots go back to the unfortunate temporal overlap of Arab and Jewish nationalism in the region. The failure to secure a reciprocally acceptable accommodation of these colliding movements heightens the probability of future Arab-Jewish war in the region. Many Israelis manifest surprise at the recrudescence of violence after ten years of comparative peace, following the 1956 war. (The Israeli Defense Army, to be sure, did not, but its mandate, of course, is defense and not political settlement.) Since 1967, Israelis have watched with bafflement and then indignation the growing involvement of Israeli Arabs ("our Arabs") in the Palestinian struggle.

There should be no surprise. A system of ethnic nationalism leads inevitably to the politicization of ethnic groups that either have already defined themselves sufficiently to withstand assimilation or are rejected by the major group as unfit for assimilation. The United Nations Special Committee on Palestine of 1947, dealing directly with passionate advocates for each group, was fully aware of this dynamic, and the acronymic UNSCOP majority report adopted the only strategy that would guarantee minimum order in the region: separate Jewish and Arab states in Palestine. If the Arabs bear the responsibility for frustrating this international policy in 1948, the Israelis acquired some complicity in tacit and perhaps more explicit agreements; they are certainly not doing enough, in proportion to their own security interest, now.

The official Palestinian position calls for the disman-
tling of the Jewish state and the creation of a secular state
in which Arabs and Jews will be equal and in which civic
rights and obligations will ensue without regard to ethnic
or religious identity. This is one of those droll symmetries
that one quickly learns to expect in the Middle East: the
Palestinian position vis-à-vis Israeli Jews is simply an
inversion of the Israeli Jew's perspective vis-à-vis the Palestinian Arab. Just as the Israeli elite has refused to recognize the genuine *national* aspirations of the Palestinians, the Palestinians have refused to accept the national
aspirations of the Israelis. Whatever their antecedent
nationalities, Israelis are not Polish and Moroccan Jews,
and Palestinians are not South Syrians. Arabs and Jews
have been bitten by the bug and have succumbed to a
severe case of nationalism; neither group is going to settle
for any solution that in the aggregate gives it no more
than institutional minority guarantees within the state of
an alien majority. In the limited context of Palestine, the
possibility of an accommodation between Arab and Jew
cannot even be imagined without a reciprocal recognition
of these facts. Zionism is no more an imposed European
creation than is Palestinian nationalism an artificial strategy devised by Nasser or the Kremlin. Each of these
movements has arisen from intense and indigenous group
demands, and the dynamic continues there and not
abroad.

The attractiveness of the official Palestinian position
derives from a number of features, not the least of which
is a growing weariness with the frightening parochialism
and parochializing effect of the nation-state (especially
when it is not one's own state). To be sure, the institu-

tionalized process that we learn to symbolize and mythologize as the state is not a natural phenomenon; it is a cultural artifact that can be used or scrapped according to the needs of justice and social order. But the current problems in the Middle East are not really of this metapolitical tenor. The crucial challenge is the creation of community structures that fulfill the needs of the individuals in the region in a manner compatible with minimum order and human dignity. The Palestinian position simply does not offer this. Whether or not their position is genuine and not merely tactical (the Palestinian characterization of Lebanon as an "artificial state" makes it seem that it is not genuine), it is not the best policy: it is obviously unacceptable to Israel and, if effected, promises all the domestic tranquility of Cyprus and Northern Ireland. But even considering it as a hypothesis forces one to come to terms with the ultimate gravamen of the Arab-Israeli struggle. The Arab-Israeli dispute is indeed susceptible to the grand language of international politics and ideological conflict of territorial expansion and national security. But its substratum is a persisting psychological inability, on the part of Arabs and Jews, to trust each other and ultimately to see each other as neither more nor less than human. One cannot generalize about Arab or Jewish views, for there are major differences on elite and rank-and-file levels of each group; moreover, each individual's views, however affected by the official line, are most decisively shaped by his own experience. Nevertheless, official views, promoted by elites through various media, do suggest reciprocal interlocking misperceptions of Arab and Jew, reflecting, in each case, a type of collective neurosis that becomes self-fulfilling as leaders act to structure reality so that it conforms to their own anxieties. To put it crudely: the Arabs seem to require a proximate colonialist, while the Israelis require a proximate anti-Semite. Adversarial acts will be regularly poured into these procrustean molds.

There is probably no other patch on the globe where groups that believe they are locked in a life-and-death struggle so persistently assure outsiders that they do not hate each other. The frequency and intensity with which these affirmations of brotherly love are volunteered controvert the impression they seek to convey. It is painfully patent that Israelis and Arabs do hate and fear each other and that members of each group harbor insecurities that color and tone the world they view. One need not equate the experiences of being a Jew or being an Arab in order to sense the deep insecurities of each and the reciprocal conjunction they have found. Many Israelis do indeed feel "superior" to Arabs, and many Arabs do feel a sense of personal and group worthlessness; these perceptions are quite interchangeable. Human beings who compulsively relate themselves toward others in terms of superordination or subordination are feeding a personal and social illness. The tensions generated often result in exuberant nationalism or violence, and they are regularly accompanied by a clear model of "the enemy."

The deeper symmetry if not identity of these reciprocal national incubi is more apparent to observers than to Middle Easterners themselves. Ahmed Shukairy, until 1967 the leader of the Palestinians, is indeed an Arab, but he and his venal demagoguery are no more representative of the Palestinian or Egyptian viewpoint than is the most rabid territorial expansionist in Israel representative of the Jews. The transformation of group hatred into violence cannot be monopolized; members of all different groups in the Middle East have committed atrocities, which were stimulated and justified in terms of the overriding threat of group destruction. Each atrocity, in turn, has raised the level of mutual fear and reciprocal hostility a notch higher.

If technological development in the Middle East is jaggedly uneven from state to state, psychological underdevelopment in the region is distressingly uniform. In a number of existential features, this cradle of civilization reflects some deep primevalism.

> . . . man made his appearance on the face of the earth in tiny social units whose relation to similar units was dominated by fear and hostility. When homo sapiens came into view about half a million years ago his wandering bands were in deadly peril from other species and especially from proto-human rivals. Parochialism, self-sacrifice, and the expectation of violence were perspectives that enabled man to live; and they persist to this day.[*]

Contemporary Middle Eastern nationalism is, in many ways, no more than a streamlined carrier for this prehistoric syndrome, with stereotypes hauled from the past and pressed into new service. But in the interdependent world of the modern Middle East, they no longer serve group interests; they threaten the future of group, regional, and perhaps global existence.

The stereotypes must be seen for what they are. But

[*] M. McDougal, H. Lasswell, and I. Vlasic, *Law and Public Order in Space* (New Haven: Yale University Press, 1963), p. 46.

each has become an important base of elite power and, indeed, national consciousness, and they are not likely to be readily abandoned. Over time they may be chipped away by interaction, at all levels of society. It is only intimacy that can ultimately strip off the cultural artifacts of Arab and Jew and reveal—human beings. Open arenas such as Jerusalem and vehicles of porous interaction such as the SDT may accelerate this process.

Although ultimate change must come from within, it now seems clear that the *initiation* of a process of change must come from outside the region. Indigenous doctrines of Shalom, Salaam, and Islam abound. From a rhetorical standpoint, the best political speeches have always come from the Middle East; the region is rich in able politicians, smart tacticians, and sonorous demagogues. Unfortunately, it lacks statesmen. No leader in the Middle East has been able to rise above his ethnicism, tribalism, nationalism, or more occult and sublime brand of mysticism to see and to identify himself with the genuine needs and real aspirations of the peoples of the region. Middle Eastern cosmopolitanism—Israeli and Arab—is levantine: a matter of form and not of substance. The Oxbridge or Parisian accent of the speaker conceals the narrowest and most brittle of group perspectives. These perspectives may well have been shaped in a past in which they had coherence, but external changes have transformed them into instruments of self-destruction.

The crucial relevance of psycho-personal factors to individual and group political behavior are appreciated on the theoretical level, but it is exceedingly difficult to frame, let alone to apply, some form of therapy. Yet the real problem in the Middle East is neither territorial nor ideological; it is the continuous inculcation and reinforcement of parochial subjectivities that cannot tolerate coexistence with others. From Gemini XI, it is clear that Arab, Sunni and Shi'i, Jew, Druze, Kurd, and Copt do indeed live cheek by jowl in the comparatively small region of the Middle East, just as it is clear that black man and white man live together in the United States. In the Middle East, as in the United States, it is necessary that inhabitants simply recognize and come to terms with a fact.

Macropsychotherapy is not yet feasible, but the lysis of generations holds great promise. If the Middle East can be politically structured so that for the present combat is too costly, a new generation that knew not Pharoah may emerge and be shaped by transnational communication. As technology shrinks the globe, peace ships and satellites can create a universal image of man and obsolesce political boundaries.

In the short run, the global danger must be appreciated. The geographical location of the Middle East and the general level of interdependence in the world necessarily transform and extend conflict in that region into a threat to world peace and, hence, a matter of global concern. The Middle East crisis carries us beyond the conveniently malleable label of "moral concern" to the abrupt realization that we inhabit a global village; a conflagration in any part of it can hurt and even destroy the rest. This does not imply that other states should or can dictate a solution. It does mean that they are, perforce, participants and that they need not be the least bit defensive about their concern in clarifying a policy for that area. The first part of wisdom will be a clear perception of the facts.

The area must be recognized for what it is: a regional multipolar arena, which will continue to be unstable because of fragmentary development and the ambitious and conflicting political goals of various national elites there. The appropriate goal for Power diplomacy, then, is to help create the conditions for minimum order in the region, to lower the level of overt violence, to isolate or neutralize the initiators of unrest, and to resolve the major moral and human problem—the plight of the Palestine refugees—in the most equitable manner possible. These operations must be carried out by drawing upon local cooperation where it is available and skirting the short-sighted obstinance of a number of elite groups. There is, at least for the time being, a convergence of Great Power interest; no Power seeks a recrudescence of violence in the Middle East, and all are coming to the realization that their present courses can only lead to the gravest of collisions. Within the limits of feasibility and possibility, there is now room for creative diplomacy. If the rewards for success here are not great, the penalty for failure may be enormous.

APPENDIX

The documents collected here should not be viewed as an exhaustive or even selective survey of the political communications of the Middle East. They represent, instead, the major international statements of policy since 1920 regarding the problem complex of Palestine. The reader's attention is directed to the startling uniformities in international policy over the past fifty years.

The League of Nations' Palestine Mandate
(July 24, 1922)

"The Council of the League of Nations:

Whereas the Principal Allied Powers have agreed, for the purpose of giving effect to the provisions of Article 22 of the Covenant of the League of Nations, to entrust to a Mandatory selected by the said Powers the administration of the territory of Palestine, which formerly belonged to the Turkish Empire, within such boundaries as may be fixed by them; and

Whereas the Principal Allied Powers have also agreed that the Mandatory should be responsible for putting into effect the declaration originally made on November 2nd, 1917, by the Government of His Britannic Majesty, and adopted by the said Powers, in favour of the establishment in Palestine of a national home for the Jewish people, it being clearly understood that nothing should be done which might prejudice the civil and religious rights of existing non-Jewish communities in Palestine, or the rights and political status enjoyed by Jews in any other country; and

Whereas recognition has thereby been given to the historical connexion of the Jewish people with Palestine and to the grounds for reconstituting their national home in that country; and

Whereas the Principal Allied Powers have selected His Britannic Majesty as the Mandatory for Palestine; and

Whereas the mandate in respect of Palestine has been formulated in the following terms and submitted to the Council of the League for approval; and

Whereas His Britannic Majesty has accepted the mandate in respect of Palestine and undertaken to exercise it on behalf of the League of Nations in conformity with the following provisions; and

Whereas by the aforementioned Article 22 (paragraph 8), it is provided that the degree of authority, control or administration to be exercised by the Mandatory, not having been previously agreed upon by the Members of the League, shall be explicitly defined by the Council of the League of Nations;

Confirming the said Mandate, defines its terms as follows:

ARTICLE 1

The Mandatory shall have full powers of legislation and of administration, save as they may be limited by the terms of this mandate.

ARTICLE 2

The Mandatory shall be responsible for placing the country under such political, administrative and economic conditions as will secure the establishment of the Jewish national home, as laid down in the preamble, and the development of self-governing institutions, and also for safeguarding the civil and religious rights of all the inhabitants of Palestine, irrespective of race and religion.

ARTICLE 3

The Mandatory shall, so far as circumstances permit, encourage local autonomy.

ARTICLE 4

An appropriate Jewish agency shall be recognized as a public body for the purpose of advising and cooperating with the Administration of Palestine in such economic, social and other matters as may affect the establishment of the Jewish national home and the interests of the Jewish population in Palestine, and, subject always to the control of the Administration, to assist and take part in the development of the country.

The Zionist Organization, so long as its organization and constitution are in the opinion of the Mandatory appropriate, shall be recognized as such agency. It shall take steps in consultation with His Britannic Majesty's Government to secure the co-operation of all Jews who are willing to assist in the establishment of the Jewish national home.

ARTICLE 5

The Mandatory shall be responsible for seeing that no Palestine territory shall be ceded or leased to, or in any way placed under the control of, the Government of any foreign Power.

ARTICLE 6

The Administration of Palestine, while ensuring that the rights and position of other sections of the population are not prejudiced, shall facilitate Jewish immigration under suitable conditions and shall encourage, in co-operation with the Jewish agency referred to in Article 4, close settlement by Jews on the land, including State lands and waste lands not required for public purposes.

ARTICLE 7

The Administration of Palestine shall be responsible for enacting a nationality law. There shall be included in this law provisions framed so as to facilitate the acquisition of Palestinian citizenship by Jews who take up their permanent residence in Palestine.

ARTICLE 8

The privileges and immunities of foreigners, including the benefits of consular jurisdiction and protection as formerly enjoyed by Capitulation or usage in the Ottoman Empire, shall not be applicable in Palestine.

Unless the Powers whose nationals enjoyed the aforementioned privileges and immunities on August 1st, 1914, shall have previously renounced the right to their re-establishment, or shall have agreed to their non-application for a specified period, these privileges and immunities shall, at the expiration of the mandate, be immediately re-established in their entirety or with such modifications as may have been agreed upon between the Powers concerned.

ARTICLE 9

The Mandatory shall be responsible for seeing that the judicial system established in Palestine shall assure to foreigners, as well as to natives, a complete guarantee of their rights.

Respect for the personal status of the various peoples and communities and for their religious interests shall be fully guaranteed. In particular, the control and administration of Waqfs shall be exercised in accordance with religious law and the dispositions of the founders.

ARTICLE 10

Pending the making of special extradition agreements relating to Palestine, the extradition treaties in force between the Mandatory and other foreign Powers shall apply to Palestine.

ARTICLE 11

The Administration of Palestine shall take all necessary measures to safeguard the interests of the community in connection with the development of the country, and, subject to any international obligations accepted by the Mandatory, shall have full power to provide for public ownership or control of any of the natural resources of the country or of the public works, services and utilities established or to be established therein. It shall introduce a land system appropriate to the needs of the country having regard, among other things, to the desirability of promoting the close settlement and intensive cultivation of the land.

The Administration may arrange with the Jewish agency mentioned in Article 4 to construct or operate, upon fair and equitable terms, any public works, services and utilities, and to develop any of the natural resources of the country, in so far as these matters are not directly undertaken by the Administration. Any such arrangements shall provide that no profits distributed by such agency, directly or indirectly, shall exceed a reasonable rate of interest on the capital, and any further profits shall be utilized by it for the benefit of the country in a manner approved by the Administration.

ARTICLE 12

The Mandatory shall be entrusted with the control of the foreign relations of Palestine, and the right to issue exequaturs to consuls appointed by foreign Powers. He shall also be entitled to afford diplomatic and consular protection to citizens of Palestine when outside its territorial limits.

ARTICLE 13

All responsibility in connexion with the Holy Places and religious buildings or sites in Palestine, including that of preserving existing rights and of securing free access to the Holy Places, religious buildings and sites and the free exercise of worship, while ensuring the requirements of public order and decorum, is assumed by the Mandatory, who shall be responsible solely to the League of Nations in all matters connected herewith, provided that nothing in this article shall prevent the Mandatory from entering into such arrangements as he may deem reasonable with the Administration for the purpose of carrying the provisions of this article into effect; and provided also that nothing in this Mandate shall be construed as conferring upon the Mandatory authority to interfere with the fabric or the management of purely Moslem sacred shrines, the immunities of which are guaranteed.

ARTICLE 14

A special Commission shall be appointed by the Mandatory to study, define and determine the rights and claims in connection with the Holy Places and the rights and claims relating to the different religious communities in Palestine. The method of nomination, the composition and the functions of this Commission shall be submitted to the Council of the League for its approval, and the Commission shall not be appointed or enter upon its functions without the approval of the Council.

ARTICLE 15

The Mandatory shall see that complete freedom of conscience and the free exercise of all forms of worship, subject only to the maintenance of public order and morals are ensured to all. No discrimination of any kind shall be made between the inhabitants of Palestine on the ground of race, religion or language. No person shall be excluded from Palestine on the sole ground of his religious belief.

The right of each community to maintain its own schools for the education of its own members in its own language, while conforming to such educational requirements of a general nature as the Administration may impose, shall not be denied or impaired.

ARTICLE 16

The Mandatory shall be responsible for exercising such supervision over religious or eleemosynary bodies of all faiths in Palestine as may be required for the maintenance of public order and good government. Subject to such supervision, no measures shall be taken in Palestine to obstruct or interfere with the enterprise of such bodies or to discriminate against any representative or member of them on the ground of his religion or nationality.

ARTICLE 17

The Administration of Palestine may organize on a voluntary basis the forces necessary for the preservation of peace and order, and also for the defence of the country, subject, however, to the supervision of the Mandatory, but shall not use them for purposes other than those above specified save with the consent of the Mandatory. Except for such purposes, no military, naval or air forces shall be raised or maintained by the Administration of Palestine.

Nothing in this article shall preclude the Administration of Palestine from contributing to the cost of the maintenance of the forces of the Mandatory in Palestine.

The Mandatory shall be entitled at all times to use the roads, railways and ports of Palestine for the movement of armed forces and the carriage of fuel and supplies.

ARTICLE 18

The Mandatory shall see that there is no discrimination in Palestine against the nationals of any State Member of the League of Nations (including companies incorporated under its laws) as compared with those of the Mandatory or of any foreign State in matters concerning taxation, commerce or navigation, the exercise of industries or professions, or in the treatment of merchant vessels or civil aircraft. Similarly, there shall be no discrimination in Palestine against goods originating in or destined for any of the said States, and there shall be freedom of transit under equitable conditions across the mandated area.

Subject as aforesaid and to the other provisions of this mandate, the Administration of Palestine may, on the advice of the Mandatory, impose such taxes and customs duties as it may consider necessary, and take such steps as it may think best to promote the development of the natural resources of the country and to safeguard the interests of the population. It may also, on the advice of the Mandatory, conclude a special customs agreement with any State the territory of which in 1914 was wholly included in Asiatic Turkey or Arabia.

ARTICLE 19

The Mandatory shall adhere on behalf of the Administration of Palestine to any general international conventions already existing, or which may be concluded hereafter with the approval of the League of Nations, respecting the slave traffic, the traffic in arms and ammunition, or the traffic in drugs, or relating to commercial equality, freedom of transit and navigation, aerial navigation and postal, telegraphic and wireless communication or literary, artistic or industrial property.

ARTICLE 20

The Mandatory shall co-operate on behalf of the Administration of Palestine, so far as religious, social and other conditions may permit, in the execution of any common policy adopted by the League of Nations for preventing and combating disease, including diseases of plants and animals.

ARTICLE 21

The Mandatory shall secure the enactment within twelve months from this date, and shall ensure the execution of a

Law of Antiquities based on the following rules. This law shall ensure equality of treatment in the matter of excavations and archaeological research to the nationals of all States Members of the League of Nations. . . .

ARTICLE 22

English, Arabic and Hebrew shall be the official languages of Palestine. Any statement or inscription in Arabic on stamps or money in Palestine shall be repeated in Hebrew and any statement or inscription in Hebrew shall be repeated in Arabic.

ARTICLE 23

The Administration of Palestine shall recognize the holy days of the respective communities in Palestine as legal days of rest for the members of such communities.

ARTICLE 24

The Mandatory shall make to the Council of the League of Nations an annual report to the satisfaction of the Council as to the measures taken during the year to carry out the provisions of the mandate. Copies of all laws and regulations promulgated or issued during the year shall be communicated with the report.

ARTICLE 25

In the territories lying between the Jordan and the eastern boundary of Palestine as ultimately determined, the Mandatory shall be entitled, with the consent of the Council of the League of Nations, to postpone or withhold application of such provisions of this mandate as he may consider inapplicable to the existing local conditions, and to make such provision for the administration of the territories as he may consider suitable to those conditions, provided that no action shall be taken which is inconsistent with the provisions of Articles 15, 16 and 18.

ARTICLE 26

The Mandatory agrees that if any dispute whatever should arise between the Mandatory and another Member of the

League of Nations relating to the interpretation or the application of the provisions of the mandate, such dispute, if it cannot be settled by negotiation, shall be submitted to the Permanent Court of International Justice provided for by Article 14 of the Covenant of the League of Nations.

ARTICLE 27

The consent of the Council of the League of Nations is required for any modification of the terms of this mandate.

ARTICLE 28

In the event of the termination of the mandate hereby conferred upon the Mandatory, the Council of the League of Nations shall make such arrangements as may be deemed necessary for safeguarding in perpetuity, under guarantee of the League, the rights secured by Articles 13 and 14, and shall use its influence for securing, under the guarantee of the League, that the Government of Palestine will fully honour the financial obligations legitimately incurred by the Administration of Palestine during the period of the mandate, including the rights of public servants to pensions or gratuities.

The present instrument shall be deposited in original in the archives of the League of Nations and certified copies shall be forwarded by the Secretary General of the League of Nations to all Members of the League.

DONE AT LONDON the twenty-fourth day of July, one thousand nine hundred and twenty-two."

The General Assembly's Resolution on the Future Government of Palestine

(November 29, 1947)

"*The General Assembly,*

"*Having met* in special session at the request of the mandatory Power to constitute and instruct a special committee to prepare for the consideration of the question of the future government of Palestine at the second regular session;

"*Having constituted* a Special Committee and instructed it to investigate all questions and issues relevant to the problem of Palestine, and to prepare proposals for the solution of the problem, and

"*Having received and examined* the report of the Special Committee (document A/364) including a number of unanimous recommendations and a plan of partition with economic union approved by the majority of the Special Committee,

"*Considers* that the present situation in Palestine is one which is likely to impair the general welfare and friendly relations among nations;

"*Takes note* of the declaration by the mandatory Power that it plans to complete its evacuation of Palestine by 1 August 1948;

"*Recommends* to the United Kingdom, as the mandatory Power for Palestine, and to all other Members of the United Nations the adoption and implementation, with regard to the future government of Palestine, of the Plan of Partition with Economic Union set out below;

"*Requests* that

"(*a*) The Security Council take the necessary measures as provided for in the plan for its implementation;

"(*b*) The Security Council consider, if circumstances during the transitional period require such consideration, whether the situation in Palestine constitutes a threat to the peace. If it decides that such a threat exists, and in order to maintain international peace and security, the Security Council should supplement the authorization of the General Assembly by taking measures, under Articles 39 and 41 of the Charter, to empower the United Nations Commission, as provided in this resolution, to exercise in Palestine the functions which are assigned to it by this resolution;

"(*c*) The Security Council determine as a threat to the peace, breach of the peace or act of aggression, in accordance with Article 39 of the Charter, any attempt to alter by force the settlement envisaged by this resolution;

"(*d*) The Trusteeship Council be informed of the responsibilities envisaged for it in this plan;

"*Calls upon* the inhabitants of Palestine to take such steps as may be necessary on their part to put this plan into effect;

"*Appeals* to all Governments and all peoples to refrain from taking any action which might hamper or delay the carrying out of these recommendations, and

"*Authorizes* the Secretary-General to reimburse travel and subsistence expenses of the members of the Commission referred to in Part I, Section B, paragraph 1 below, on such basis and in such form as he may determine most appropriate in the circumstances, and to provide the Commission with the necessary staff to assist in carrying out the functions assigned to the Commission by the General Assembly."

PLAN OF PARTITION WITH ECONOMIC UNION
PART I.—FUTURE CONSTITUTION AND GOVERNMENT OF PALESTINE

A. Termination of Mandate, Partition and Independence

1. The Mandate for Palestine shall terminate as soon as possible but in any case not later than 1 August 1948.

2. The armed forces of the mandatory Power shall be progressively withdrawn from Palestine, the withdrawal to be completed as soon as possible but in any case not later than 1 August 1948.

The mandatory Power shall advise the Commission, as far in advance as possible, of its intention to terminate the Mandate and to evacuate each area.

The mandatory Power shall use its best endeavours to ensure that an area situated in the territory of the Jewish State, including a seaport and hinterland adequate to provide facilities for a substantial immigration, shall be evacuated at the earliest possible date and in any event not later than 1 February 1948.

3. Independent Arab and Jewish States and the Special International Regime for the City of Jerusalem, set forth in part III of this plan, shall come into existence in Palestine two months after the evacuation of the armed forces of the mandatory Power has been completed but in any case not later than 1 October 1948. The boundaries of the Arab State, the Jewish State, and the City of Jerusalem shall be described in parts II and III below.

4. The period between the adoption by the General Assembly of its recommendation on the question of Palestine and the establishment of the independence of the Arab and Jewish States shall be a transitional period.

B. Steps Preparatory to Independence

1. A Commission shall be set up consisting of one representative of each of five Member States. The Members represented on the Commission shall be elected by the General

[102]

Assembly on as broad a basis, geographically and otherwise, as possible.

2. The administration of Palestine shall, as the mandatory Power withdraws its armed forces, be progressively turned over to the Commission, which shall act in conformity with the recommendations of the General Assembly, under the guidance of the Security Council. The mandatory Power shall to the fullest possible extent co-ordinate its plans for withdrawal with the plans of the Commission to take over and administer areas which have been evacuated.

In the discharge of this administrative responsibility the Commission shall have authority to issue necessary regulations and take other measures as required.

The mandatory Power shall not take any action to prevent, obstruct or delay the implementation by the Commission of the measures recommended by the General Assembly.

3. On its arrival in Palestine the Commission shall proceed to carry out measures for the establishment of the frontiers of the Arab and Jewish States and the City of Jerusalem in accordance with the general lines of the recommendations of the General Assembly on the partition of Palestine. Nevertheless, the boundaries as described in part II of this plan are to be modified in such a way that village areas as a rule will not be divided by state boundaries unless pressing reasons make that necessary.

4. The Commission, after consultation with the democratic parties and other public organizations of the Arab and Jewish States, shall select and establish in each State as rapidly as possible a Provisional Council of Government. The activities of both the Arab and Jewish Provisional Councils of Government shall be carried out under the general direction of the Commission.

If by 1 April 1948 a Provisional Council of Government cannot be selected for either of the States, or, if selected, cannot carry out its functions, the Commission shall communicate that fact to the Security Council for such action with respect to that State as the Security Council may deem proper, and to the

Secretary-General for communication to the Members of the United Nations.

5. Subject to the provisions of these recommendations, during the transitional period the Provisional Councils of Government, acting under the Commission, shall have full authority in the areas under their control, including authority over matters of immigration and land regulation.

6. The Provisional Council of Government of each State, acting under the Commission, shall progressively receive from the Commission full responsibility for the administration of that State in the period between the termination of the Mandate and the establishment of the State's independence.

7. The Commission shall instruct the Provisional Councils of Government of both the Arab and Jewish States, after their formation, to proceed to the establishment of administrative organs of government, central and local.

8. The Provisional Council of Government of each State shall, within the shortest time possible, recruit an armed militia from the residents of that State, sufficient in number to maintain internal order and to prevent frontier clashes.

This armed militia in each State shall, for operational purposes, be under the command of Jewish or Arab officers resident in that State, but general political and military control, including the choice of the militia's High Command, shall be exercised by the Commission.

9. The Provisional Council of Government of each State shall, not later than two months after the withdrawal of the armed forces of the mandatory Power, hold elections to the Constituent Assembly which shall be conducted on democratic lines.

The election regulations in each State shall be drawn up by the Provisional Council of Government and approved by the Commission. Qualified voters for each State for this election shall be persons over eighteen years of age who are: (a) Palestinian citizens residing in that State and (b) Arabs and Jews residing in the State, although not Palestinian citizens, who, before voting, have signed a notice of intention to become citizens of such State.

Arabs and Jews residing in the City of Jerusalem who have signed a notice of intention to become citizens, the Arabs of the Arab State and the Jews of the Jewish State, shall be entitled to vote in the Arab and Jewish States respectively.

Women may vote and be elected to the Constituent Assemblies.

During the transitional period no Jew shall be permitted to establish residence in the area of the proposed Arab State, and no Arab shall be permitted to establish residence in the area of the proposed Jewish State, except by special leave of the Commission.

10. The Constituent Assembly of each State shall draft a democratic constitution for its State and choose a provisional government to succeed the Provisional Council of Government appointed by the Commission. The constitutions of the States shall embody chapters 1 and 2 of the Declaration provided for in section C below and include *inter alia* provisions for:

(*a*) Establishing in each State a legislative body elected by universal suffrage and by secret ballot on the basis of proportional representation, and an executive body responsible to the legislature;

(*b*) Settling all international disputes in which the State may be involved by peaceful means in such a manner that international peace and security, and justice, are not endangered;

(*c*) Accepting the obligation of the State to refrain in its international relations from the threat or use of force against the territorial integrity or political independence of any State, or in any other manner inconsistent with the purposes of the United Nations;

(*d*) Guaranteeing to all persons equal and nondiscriminatory rights in civil, political, economic and religious matters and the enjoyment of human rights and fundamental freedoms, including freedom of religion, language, speech and publication, education, assembly and association;

(*e*) Preserving freedom of transit and visit for all residents and citizens of the other State in Palestine and the City of Jerusalem, subject to considerations of national security, provided that each State shall control residence within its borders.

11. The Commission shall appoint a preparatory economic commission of three members to make whatever arrangements are possible for economic co-operation, with a view to establishing, as soon as practicable, the Economic Union and the Joint Economic Board, as provided in section D below.

12. During the period between the adoption of the recommendations on the question of Palestine by the General Assembly and the termination of the Mandate, the mandatory Power in Palestine shall maintain full responsibility for administration in areas from which it has not withdrawn its armed forces. The Commission shall assist the mandatory Power in the carrying out of these functions. Similarly the mandatory Power shall co-operate with the Commission in the execution of its functions.

13. With a view to ensuring that there shall be continuity in the functioning of administrative services and that, on the withdrawal of the armed forces of the mandatory Power, the whole administration shall be in charge of the Provisional Councils and the Joint Economic Board, respectively, acting under the Commission, there shall be a progressive transfer, from the mandatory Power to the Commission, of responsibility for all the functions of government, including that of maintaining law and order in the areas from which the forces of the mandatory Power have been withdrawn.

14. The Commission shall be guided in its activities by the recommendations of the General Assembly and by such instructions as the Security Council may consider necessary to issue.

The measures taken by the Commission, within the recommendations of the General Assembly, shall become immediately effective unless the Commission has previously received contrary instructions from the Security Council.

The Commission shall render periodic monthly progress reports, or more frequently if desirable, to the Security Council.

15. The Commission shall make its final report to the next regular session of the General Assembly and to the Security Council simultaneously.

C. Declaration

A declaration shall be made to the United Nations by the provisional government of each proposed State before independence. It shall contain *inter alia* the following clauses:

General Provision

The stipulations contained in the declaration are recognized as fundamental laws of the State and no law, regulation or official action shall conflict or interfere with these stipulations, nor shall any law, regulation or official action prevail over them.

CHAPTER I.—HOLY PLACES, RELIGIOUS BUILDINGS AND SITES

1. Existing rights in respect of Holy Places and religious buildings or sites shall not be denied or impaired.

2. In so far as Holy Places are concerned, the liberty of access, visit and transit shall be guaranteed, in conformity with existing rights, to all residents and citizens of the other State and of the City of Jerusalem, as well as to aliens, without distinction as to nationality, subject to requirements of national security, public order and decorum.

Similarly, freedom of worship shall be guaranteed in conformity with existing rights, subject to the maintenance of public order and decorum.

3. Holy Places and religious buildings or sites shall be preserved. No act shall be permitted which may in any way impair their sacred character. If at any time it appears to the Government that any particular Holy Place, religious building or site is in need of urgent repair, the Government may call upon the community or communities concerned to carry out such

repair. The Government may carry it out itself at the expense of the community or communities concerned if no action is taken within a reasonable time.

4. No taxation shall be levied in respect of any Holy Place, religious building or site which was exempt from taxation on the date of the creation of the State.

No change in the incidence of such taxation shall be made which would either discriminate between the owners or occupiers of Holy Places, religious buildings or sites, or would place such owners or occupiers in a position less favourable in relation to the general incidence of taxation than existed at the time of the adoption of the Assembly's recommendations.

5. The Governor of the City of Jerusalem shall have the right to determine whether the provisions of the Constitution of the State in relation to Holy Places, religious buildings and sites within the borders of the State and the religious rights appertaining thereto, are being properly applied and respected, and to make decisions on the basis of existing rights in cases of disputes which may arise between the different religious communities or the rites of a religious community with respect to such places, buildings and sites. He shall receive full cooperation and such privileges and immunities as are necessary for the exercise of his functions in the State.

CHAPTER 2.—RELIGIOUS AND MINORITY RIGHTS

1. Freedom of conscience and the free exercise of all forms of worship, subject only to the maintenance of public order and morals, shall be ensured to all.

2. No discrimination of any kind shall be made between the inhabitants on the ground of race, religion, language or sex.

3. All persons within the jurisdiction of the State shall be entitled to equal protection of the laws.

4. The family law and personal status of the various minorities and their religious interests, including endowments, shall be respected.

5. Except as may be required for the maintenance of public order and good government, no measure shall be taken to

obstruct or interfere with the enterprise of religious or charitable bodies of all faiths or to discriminate against any representative or member of these bodies on the ground of his religion or nationality.

6. The State shall ensure adequate primary and secondary education for the Arab and Jewish minority, respectively, in its own language and its cultural traditions.

The right of each community to maintain its own schools for the education of its own members in its own language, while conforming to such educational requirements of a general nature as the State may impose, shall not be denied or impaired. Foreign educational establishments shall continue their activity on the basis of their existing rights.

7. No restriction shall be imposed on the free use by any citizen of the State of any language in private intercourse, in commerce, in religion, in the Press or in publications of any kind, or at public meetings.*

8. No expropriation of land owned by an Arab in the Jewish State (by a Jew in the Arab State)† shall be allowed except for public purposes. In all cases of expropriation full compensation as fixed by the Supreme Court shall be paid previous to dispossession.

CHAPTER 3.—CITIZENSHIP, INTERNATIONAL CONVENTIONS AND FINANCIAL OBLIGATIONS

1. *Citizenship.* Palestinian citizens residing in Palestine outside the City of Jerusalem, as well as Arabs and Jews who, not holding Palestinian citizenship, reside in Palestine outside the City of Jerusalem shall, upon the recognition of independence,

---

* The following stipulation shall be added to the declaration concerning the Jewish State: "In the Jewish State adequate facilities shall be given to Arabic-speaking citizens for the use of their language, either orally or in writing, in the legislature, before the Courts and in the administration."

† In the declaration concerning the Arab State, the words "by an Arab in the Jewish State" should be replaced by the words "by a Jew in the Arab State."

become citizens of the State in which they are resident and enjoy full civil and political rights. Persons over the age of eighteen years may opt, within one year from the date of recognition of independence of the State in which they reside, for citizenship of the other State, providing that no Arab residing in the area of the proposed Arab State shall have the right to opt for citizenship in the proposed Jewish State and no Jews residing in the proposed Jewish State shall have the right to opt for citizenship in the proposed Arab State. The exercise of this right of option will be taken to include the wives and children under eighteen years of age of persons so opting.

Arabs residing in the area of the proposed Jewish State and Jews residing in the area of the proposed Arab State who have signed a notice of intention to opt for citizenship of the other State shall be eligible to vote in the elections to the Constituent Assembly of that State, but not in the elections to the Constituent Assembly of the State in which they reside.

2. *International conventions*. (*a*) The State shall be bound by all the international agreements and conventions, both general and special, to which Palestine has become a party. Subject to any right of denunciation provided for therein, such agreements and conventions shall be respected by the State throughout the period for which they were concluded.

(*b*) Any dispute about the applicability and continued validity of international conventions or treaties signed or adhered to by the mandatory Power on behalf of Palestine shall be referred to the International Court of Justice in accordance with the provisions of the Statute of the Court.

3. *Financial obligations*. (*a*) The State shall respect and fulfill all financial obligations of whatever nature assumed on behalf of Palestine by the mandatory Power during the exercise of the Mandate and recognized by the State. This provision includes the right of public servants to pensions, compensation or gratuities.

(*b*) These obligations shall be fulfilled through participation in the Joint Economic Board in respect of those obligations applicable to Palestine as a whole, and individually in respect of those applicable to, and fairly apportionable between, the States.

(c) A Court of Claims, affiliated with the Joint Economic Board, and composed of one member appointed by the United Nations, one representative of the United Kingdom and one representative of the State concerned, should be established. Any dispute between the United Kingdom and the State respecting claims not recognized by the latter should be referred to that Court.

(d) Commercial concessions granted in respect of any part of Palestine prior to the adoption of the resolution by the General Assembly shall continue to be valid according to their terms, unless modified by agreement between the concession-holder and the State.

CHAPTER 4.—MISCELLANEOUS PROVISIONS

1. The provisions of chapters 1 and 2 of the declaration shall be under the guarantee of the United Nations, and no modifications shall be made in them without the assent of the General Assembly of the United Nations. Any Member of the United Nations shall have the right to bring to the attention of the General Assembly any infraction or danger of infraction of any of these stipulations, and the General Assembly may thereupon make such recommendations as it may deem proper in the circumstances.

2. Any dispute relating to the application or the interpretation of this declaration shall be referred, at the request of either party, to the International Court of Justice, unless the parties agree to another mode of settlement.

D. Economic Union and Transit

1. The Provisional Council of Government of each State shall enter into an undertaking with respect to Economic Union and Transit. This undertaking shall be drafted by the Commission provided for in section B, paragraph 1, utilizing to the greatest possible extent the advice and co-operation of representative organizations and bodies from each of the pro-

posed States. It shall contain provisions to establish the Economic Union of Palestine and provide for other matters of common interest. If by 1 April 1948 the Provisional Councils of Government have not entered into the undertaking, the undertaking shall be put into force by the Commission.

The Economic Union of Palestine

2. The objectives of the Economic Union of Palestine shall be:

(*a*) A customs union;

(*b*) A joint currency system providing for a single foreign exchange rate;

(*c*) Operation in the common interest on a non-discriminatory basis of railways; inter-State highways; postal, telephone and telegraphic services, and ports and airports involved in international trade and commerce;

(*d*) Joint economic development, especially in respect of irrigation, land reclamation and soil conservation;

(*e*) Access for both States and for the City of Jerusalem on a non-discriminatory basis to water and power facilities.

3. There shall be established a Joint Economic Board, which shall consist of three representatives of each of the two States and three foreign members appointed by the Economic and Social Council of the United Nations. The foreign members shall be appointed in the first instance for a term of three years; they shall serve as individuals and not as representatives of States.

4. The functions of the Joint Economic Board shall be to implement either directly or by delegation the measures necessary to realize the objectives of the Economic Union. It shall have all powers of organization and administration necessary to fulfil its functions.

5. The States shall bind themselves to put into effect the decisions of the Joint Economic Board. The Board's decisions shall be taken by a majority vote.

6. In the event of failure of a State to take the necessary action the Board may, by a vote of six members, decide to

withhold an appropriate portion of that part of the customs revenue to which the State in question is entitled under the Economic Union. Should the State persist in its failure to co-operate, the Board may decide by a simple majority vote upon such further sanctions, including disposition of funds which it has withheld, as it may deem appropriate.

7. In relation to economic development, the functions of the Board shall be the planning, investigation and encouragement of joint development projects, but it shall not undertake such projects except with the assent of both States and the City of Jerusalem, in the event that Jerusalem is directly involved in the development project.

8. In regard to the joint currency system the currencies circulating in the two States and the City of Jerusalem shall be issued under the authority of the Joint Economic Board, which shall be the sole issuing authority and which shall determine the reserves to be held against such currencies.

9. So far as is consistent with paragraph 2 (*b*) above, each State may operate its own central bank, control its own fiscal and credit policy, its foreign exchange receipts and expenditures, the grant of import licenses, and may conduct international financial operations on its own faith and credit. During the first two years after the termination of the Mandate, the Joint Economic Board shall have the authority to take such measures as may be necessary to ensure that—to the extent that the total foreign exchange revenues of the two States from the export of goods and services permit, and provided that each State takes appropriate measures to conserve its own foreign exchange resources—each State shall have available, in any twelve months' period, foreign exchange sufficient to assure the supply of quantities of imported goods and services for consumption in its territory equivalent to the quantities of such goods and services consumed in that territory in the twelve months' period ending 31 December 1947.

10. All economic authority not specifically vested in the Joint Economic Board is reserved to each State.

11. There shall be a common customs tariff with complete

freedom of trade between the States, and between the States and the City of Jerusalem.

12. The tariff schedules shall be drawn up by a Tariff Commission, consisting of representatives of each of the States in equal numbers, and shall be submitted to the Joint Economic Board for approval by a majority vote. In case of disagreement in the Tariff Commission, the Joint Economic Board shall arbitrate the points of difference. In the event that the Tariff Commission fails to draw up any schedule by a date to be fixed, the Joint Economic Board shall determine the tariff schedule.

13. The following items shall be a first charge on the customs and other common revenue of the Joint Economic Board:

(*a*) The expenses of the customs service and of the operation of the joint services;

(*b*) The administrative expenses of the Joint Economic Board;

(*c*) The financial obligations of the Administration of Palestine consisting of:

(i) The service of the outstanding public debt;

(ii) The cost of superannuation benefits, now being paid or falling due in the future, in accordance with the rules and to the extent established by paragraph 3 of chapter 3 above.

14. After these obligations have been met in full, the surplus revenue from the customs and other common services shall be divided in the following manner: not less than 5 per cent and not more than 10 per cent to the City of Jerusalem; the residue shall be allocated to each State by the Joint Economic Board equitably, with the objective of maintaining a sufficient and suitable level of government and social services in each State, except that the share of either State shall not exceed the amount of that State's contribution to the revenues of the Economic Union by more than approximately four million pounds in any year. The amount granted may be adjusted by the Board according to the price level in relation to the prices prevailing at the time of the establishment of the Union. After five years, the principles of the distribution of the joint revenues may be

revised by the Joint Economic Board on a basis of equity.

15. All international conventions and treaties affecting customs tariff rates, and those communications services under the jurisdiction of the Joint Economic Board, shall be entered into by both States. In these matters, the two States shall be bound to act in accordance with the majority vote of the Joint Economic Board.

16. The Joint Economic Board shall endeavour to secure for Palestine's exports fair and equal access to world markets.

17. All enterprises operated by the Joint Economic Board shall pay fair wages on a uniform basis.

Freedom of transit and visit

18. The undertaking shall contain provisions preserving freedom of transit and visit for all residents or citizens of both States and of the City of Jerusalem, subject to security considerations; provided that each State and the City shall control residence within its borders.

Termination, modification and interpretation of the undertaking

19. The undertaking and any treaty issuing therefrom shall remain in force for a period of ten years. It shall continue in force until notice of termination, to take effect two years thereafter, is given by either of the parties.

20. During the initial ten-year period, the undertaking and any treaty issuing therefrom may not be modified except by consent of both parties and with the approval of the General Assembly.

21. Any dispute relating to the application or the interpretation of the undertaking and any treaty issuing therefrom shall be referred, at the request of either party, to the International Court of Justice, unless the parties agree to another mode of settlement.

E. Assets

1. The movable assets of the Administration of Palestine shall be allocated to the Arab and Jewish States and the City

of Jerusalem on an equitable basis. Allocations should be made by the United Nations Commission referred to in section B, paragraph 1, above. Immovable assets shall become the property of the government of the territory in which they are situated.

2. During the period between the appointment of the United Nations Commission and the termination of the Mandate, the mandatory Power shall, except in respect of ordinary operations, consult with the commission on any measure which it may contemplate involving the liquidation, disposal or encumbering of the assets of the Palestine Government, such as the accumulated treasury surplus, the proceeds of Government bond issues, State lands or any other asset.

F. Admission to Membership in the United Nations

When the independence of either the Arab or the Jewish State as envisaged in this plan has become effective and the declaration and undertaking, as envisaged in this plan, have been signed by either of them, sympathetic consideration should be given to its application for admission to membership in the United Nations in accordance with Article 4 of the Charter of the United Nations.

PART II.—BOUNDARIES*

A. The Arab State

The area of the Arab State in Western Galilee is bounded on the west by the Mediterranean and on the north by the frontier of the Lebanon from Ras en Naqura to a point north of Saliha. From there the boundary proceeds southwards, leaving the built-up area of Saliha in the Arab State, to join the

* The boundary lines described in part II are indicated in Annex A [not included here]. The base map used in marking and describing this boundary is "Palestine 1:250,000" published by the Survey of Palestine, 1946.

southernmost point of this village. Thence it follows the western boundary line of the villages of 'Alma, Rihaniya and Teitaba, thence following the northern boundary line of Meirun village to join the Acre-Safad sub-district boundary line. It follows this line to a point west of Es Sammu'i village and joins it again at the northernmost point of Farradiya. Thence it follows the sub-district boundary line to the Acre-Safad main road. From here it follows the western boundary of Kafr I'nan village until it reaches the Tiberias-Acre sub-district boundary line, passing to the west of the junction of the Acre-Safad and Lubiya-Kafr I'nan roads. From the south-west corner of Kafr I'nan village the boundary line follows the western boundary of the Tiberias sub-district to a point close to the boundary line between the villages of Maghar and Eilabun, thence bulging out to the west to include as much of the eastern part of the plain of Battuf as is necessary for the reservoir proposed by the Jewish Agency for the irrigation of lands to the south and east.

The boundary rejoins the Tiberias sub-district boundary at a point on the Nazareth-Tiberias road south-east of the built-up area of Tur'an; thence it runs southwards, at first following the sub-district boundary and then passing between the Kadoorie Agricultural School and Mount Tabor, to a point due south at the base of Mount Tabor. From here it runs due west, parallel to the horizontal grid line 230, to the north-east corner of the village lands of Tel Adashim. It then runs to the north-west corner of these lands, when it turns south and west so as to include in the Arab State the sources of the Nazareth water supply in Yafa village. On reaching Ginneiger it follows the eastern, northern and western boundaries of the lands of this village to their south-west corner, whence it proceeds in a straight line to a point on the Haifa-Afula railway on the boundary between the villages of Sarid and El Mujeidil. This is the point of intersection.

The south-western boundary of the area of the Arab State in Galilee takes a line from this point, passing northwards along the eastern boundaries of Sarid and Gevat to the north-eastern corner of Nahalal, proceeding thence across the land of Kefar ha Horesh to a central point on the southern boundary of the village of 'Ilut, thence westwards along that village boundary to the eastern boundary of Beit Lahm, thence northwards and north-eastwards along its western boundary to the north-eastern corner of Waldheim and thence north-westwards across the village lands of Shafa 'Amr to the south-eastern corner of Ramat Yohanan. From here it runs due north-north-east to a point on the Shafa 'Amr-Haifa road, west of its junction with the road to I'Billin. From there it proceeds north-east to a point on the southern boundary of I'Billin situated to the west of the I'Billin-Birwa road. Thence along that boundary to its westernmost point, whence it turns to the north, follows across the village land of Tamra to the north-westernmost corner and along the western boundary of Julis until it reaches the Acre-Safad road. It then runs westwards along the southern side of the Safad-Acre road to the Galilee-Haifa District boundary, from which point it follows that boundary to the sea.

The boundary of the hill country of Samaria and Judea starts on the Jordan River at the Wadi Malih south-east of Beisan and runs due west to meet the Beisan-Jericho road and then follows the western side of that road in a north-westerly direction to the junction of the boundaries of the sub-districts of Beisan, Nablus, and Jenin. From that point it follows the Nablus-Jenin sub-district boundary westwards for a distance of about three kilometres and then turns north-westwards, passing to the east of the built-up areas of the villages of Jalbun and Faqqu'a, to the boundary of the sub-districts of Jenin and Beisan at a point north-east of Nuris. Thence it proceeds first north-westwards to a point due north of the built-up area of Zir'in and then westwards to the Afula-Jenin railway, thence north-westwards along the district boundary line to the point of intersection on the Hejaz railway. From here the boundary runs south-westwards, including the built-up area and some of the land of the village of Kh.Lid in the Arab State to cross the Haifa-Jenin road at a point on the district boundary be-

tween Haifa and Samaria west of El Mansi. It follows this
boundary to the southernmost point of the village of El Butei-
mat. From here it follows the northern and eastern boundaries
of the village of Ar'ara, rejoining the Haifa-Samaria district
boundary at Wadi'Ara, and thence proceeding south-south-
westwards in an approximately straight line joining up with
the western boundary of Qaqun to a point east of the railway
line on the eastern boundary of Qaqun village. From here it
runs along the railway line some distance to the east of it to
a point just east of the Tulkarm railway station. Thence the
boundary follows a line half-way between the railway and the
Tulkarm-Qalqiliya-Jaljuliya and Ras el Ein road to a point
just east of Ras el Ein station, whence it proceeds along the
railway some distance to the east of it to the point on the railway line south of the junction of the Haifa-Lydda and Beit
Nabala lines, whence it proceeds along the southern border of
Lydda airport to its southwest corner, thence in a south-westerly direction to a point just west of the built-up area of Sara-
fand el 'Amar, whence it turns south, passing just to the west
of the built-up area of Abu el Fadil to the north-east corner
of the lands of Beer Ya'Aqov. (The boundary line should be
so demarcated as to allow direct access from the Arab State
to the airport.) Thence the boundary line follows the western
and southern boundaries of Ramle village, to the north-east
corner of El Na'ana village, thence in a straight line to the
southernmost point of El Barriya, along the eastern boundary
of that village and the southern boundary of 'Innaba village.
Thence it turns north to follow the southern side of the Jaffa-
Jerusalem road until El Qubab, whence it follows the road to
the boundary of Abu Shusha. It runs along the eastern boundaries of Abu Shusha, Seidun, Hulda to the southernmost point
of Hulda, thence westwards in a straight line to the northeast-
ern corner of Umm Kalkha, thence following the northern
boundaries of Umm Kalkha, Qazaza and the northern and
western boundaries of Mukhezin to the Gaza District boundary and thence runs across the village lands of El Mismiya,
El Kabira, and Yasur to the southern point of intersection,

which is midway between the built-up areas of Yasur and Batani Sharqi.

From the southern point of intersection the boundary line runs north-westwards between the villages of Gan Yavne and Barqa to the sea at a point half way between Nabi Yunis and Minat el Qila, and south-eastwards to a point west of Qastina, whence it turns in a south-westerly direction, passing to the east of the built-up areas of Es Sawafir, Esh Sharqiya and Ibdis. From the south-east corner of Ibdis village it runs to a point south-west of the built-up area of Beit 'Affa, crossing the Hebron-El Majdal road just to the west of the built-up area of Iraq Suweidan. Thence it proceeds southwards along the western village boundary of El Faluja to the Beersheba sub-district boundary. It then runs across the tribal lands of 'Arab el Jubarat to a point on the boundary between the sub-districts of Beersheba and Hebron north of Kh. Khuweilifa, whence it proceeds in a south-westerly direction to a point on the Beersheba-Gaza main road two kilometres to the north-west of the town. It then turns south-eastwards to reach Wadi Sab' at a point situated one kilometre to the west of it. From here it turns north-eastwards and proceeds along Wadi Sab' and along the Beersheba-Hebron road for a distance of one kilometre, whence it turns eastwards and runs in a straight line to Kh. Kuseifa to join the Beersheba-Hebron sub-district boundary. It then follows the Beersheba-Hebron boundary eastwards to a point north of Ras ez Zuweira, only departing from it so as to cut across the base of the indentation between vertical grid lines 150 and 160.

About five kilometres north-east of Ras ez Zuweira it turns north, excluding from the Arab State a strip along the coast of the Dead Sea not more than seven kilometres in depth, as far as Ein Geddi, whence it turns due east to join the Trans-jordan frontier in the Dead Sea.

The northern boundary of the Arab section of the coastal plain runs from a point between Minat el Qila and Nabi Yunis, passing between the built-up areas of Gan Yavne and

Barqa to the point of intersection. From here it turns south-westwards, running across the lands of Batani Sharqi, along the eastern boundary of the lands of Beit Daras and across the lands of Julis, leaving the built-up areas of Batani Sharqi and Julis to the westwards, as far as the north-west corner of the lands of Beit Tima. Thence it runs east of El Jiya across the village lands of El Barbara along the eastern boundaries of the villages of Beit Jirja, Deir Suneid and Dimra. From the southeast corner of Dimra the boundary passes across the lands of Beit Hanun, leaving the Jewish lands of Nir-Am to the eastwards. From the south-east corner of Beit Hanun the line runs south-west to a point south of the parallel grid line 100, then turns north-west for two kilometres, turning again in a south-westerly direction and continuing in an almost straight line to the north-west corner of the village lands of Kirbet Ikhza'a. From there it follows the boundary line of this village to its southernmost point. It then runs in a southerly direction along the vertical grid line 90 to its junction with the horizontal grid line 70. It then turns south-eastwards to Kh. el Ruheiba and then proceeds in a southerly direction to a point known as El Baha, beyond which it crosses the Beersheba-El 'Auja main road to the west of Kh. el Mushrifa. From there it joins Wadi El Zaiyatin just to the west of El Subeita. From there it turns to the north-east and then to the south-east following this wadi and passes to the east of 'Abda to join Wadi Nafkh. It then bulges to the south-west along Wadi Nafkh, Wadi Ajrim and Wadi Lassan to the point where Wadi Lassan crosses the Egyptian frontier.

The area of the Arab enclave of Jaffa consists of that part of the town-planning area of Jaffa which lies to the west of the Jewish quarters lying south of Tel-Aviv, to the west of the continuation of Herzl street up to its junction with the Jaffa-Jerusalem road, to the south-west of the section of the Jaffa-Jerusalem road lying south-east of that junction, to the west of Miqve Yisrael lands, to the north-west of Holon local council area, to the north of the line linking up the north-west corner of Holon with the north-east corner of Bat Yam local council area and to the north of Bat Yam local council area. The question of Karton quarter will be decided by the Boundary Commission, bearing in mind among other considerations the desirability of including the smallest possible number of its Arab inhabitants and the largest possible number of its Jewish inhabitants in the Jewish State.

B. The Jewish State

The north-eastern sector of the Jewish State (Eastern Galilee) is bounded on the north and west by the Lebanese frontier and on the east by the frontiers of Syria and Transjordan. It includes the whole of the Hula Basin, Lake Tiberias, the whole of the Beisan sub-district, the boundary line being extended to the crest of the Gilboa mountains and the Wadi Malih. From there the Jewish State extends north-west, following the boundary described in respect of the Arab State.

The Jewish section of the coastal plain extends from a point between Minat et Qila and Nabi Yunis in the Gaza sub-district and includes the towns of Haifa and Tel-Aviv, leaving Jaffa as an enclave of the Arab State. The eastern frontier of the Jewish State follows the boundary described in respect of the Arab State.

The Beersheba area comprises the whole of the Beersheba sub-district, including the Negeb and the eastern part of the Gaza sub-district, but excluding the town of Beersheba and those areas described in respect of the Arab State. It includes also a strip of land along the Dead Sea stretching from the Beersheba-Hebron sub-district boundary line to Ein Geddi, as described in respect of the Arab State.

C. The City of Jerusalem

The boundaries of the City of Jerusalem are as defined in the recommendations on the City of Jerusalem. (See Part III, Section B, below.)

PART III.—CITY OF JERUSALEM

A. Special Regime

The City of Jerusalem shall be established as a *corpus separatum* under a special international regime and shall be administered by the United Nations. The Trusteeship Council shall be designated to discharge the responsibilities of the Administering Authority on behalf of the United Nations.

B. Boundaries of the City

The City of Jerusalem shall include the present municipality of Jerusalem plus the surrounding villages and towns, the most eastern of which shall be Abu Dis; the most southern, Bethlehem; the most western, Ein Karim (including also the built-up area of Motsa); and the most northern Shu-fat, as indicated on the attached sketch-map (annex B [not included here]).

C. Statute of the City

The Trusteeship Council shall, within five months of the approval of the present plan, elaborate and approve a detailed Statute of the City which shall contain *inter alia* the substance of the following provisions:

1. *Government machinery; special objectives.* The Administering Authority in discharging its administrative obligations shall pursue the following special objectives:

(*a*) To protect and to preserve the unique spiritual and religious interests located in the city of the three great monotheistic faiths throughout the world, Christian, Jewish and Moslem; to this end to ensure that order and peace, and especially religious peace, reigns in Jerusalem;

(*b*) To foster co-operation among all the inhabitants of the city in their own interests as well as in order to encourage and support the peaceful development of the mutual relations between the two Palestinian peoples throughout the Holy Land; to promote the security, well-being and any constructive measures of development of the residents, having regard to the special circumstances and customs of the various peoples and communities.

2. *Governor and administrative staff.* A Governor of the City of Jerusalem shall be appointed by the Trusteeship Council and shall be responsible to it. He shall be selected on the basis of special qualifications and without regard to nationality. He shall not, however, be a citizen of either State in Palestine.

The Governor shall represent the United Nations in the City and shall exercise on their behalf all powers of administration, including the conduct of external affairs. He shall be assisted by an administrative staff classed as international officers in the meaning of Article 100 of the Charter and chosen whenever practicable from the residents of the city and of the rest of Palestine on a non-discriminatory basis. A detailed plan for the organization of the administration of the city shall be submitted by the Governor to the Trusteeship Council and duly approved by it.

3. *Local autonomy.* (*a*) The existing local autonomous units in the territory of the city (villages, townships and municipalities) shall enjoy wide powers of local government and administration.

(*b*) The Governor shall study and submit for the consideration and decision of the Trusteeship Council a plan for the establishment of special town units consisting, respectively, of the Jewish and Arab sections of new Jerusalem. The new town units shall continue to form part of the present municipality of Jerusalem.

4. *Security measures.* (*a*) The City of Jerusalem shall be demilitarized; its neutrality shall be declared and preserved, and no para-military formations, exercises or activities shall be permitted within its borders.

(*b*) Should the administration of the City of Jerusalem be seriously obstructed or prevented by the non-co-operation or interference of one or more sections of the population, the Governor shall have authority to take such measures as may be necessary to restore the effective functioning of the administration.

(*c*) To assist in the maintenance of internal law and order and especially for the protection of the Holy Places and religious buildings and sites in the city, the Governor shall organize a special police force of adequate strength, the members of which shall be recruited outside of Palestine. The Governor shall be empowered to direct such budgetary provision as may be necessary for the maintenance of this force.

5. *Legislative organization.* A Legislative Council, elected by adult residents of the city irrespective of nationality on the basis of universal and secret suffrage and proportional representation, shall have powers of legislation and taxation. No legislative measures shall, however, conflict or interfere with the provisions which will be set forth in the Statute of the City, nor shall any law, regulation, or official action prevail over them. The Statute shall grant to the Governor a right of vetoing bills inconsistent with the provisions referred to in the preceding sentence. It shall also empower him to promulgate temporary ordinances in case the Council fails to adopt in time a bill deemed essential to the normal functioning of the administration.

6. *Administration of justice.* The Statute shall provide for the establishment of an independent judiciary system, including a court of appeal. All the inhabitants of the City shall be subject to it.

7. *Economic union and economic regime.* The City of Jerusalem shall be included in the Economic Union of Palestine and be bound by all stipulations of the undertaking and of any treaties issued therefrom, as well as by the decisions of the Joint Economic Board. The headquarters of the Economic Board shall be established in the territory of the City.

The Statute shall provide for the regulation of economic matters not falling within the regime of the Economic Union, on the basis of equal treatment and non-discrimination for all Members of the United Nations and their nationals.

[125]

8. *Freedom of transit and visit; control of residents.* Subject to considerations of security, and of economic welfare as determined by the Governor under the directions of the Trusteeship Council, freedom of entry into, and residence within, the borders of the City shall be guaranteed for the residents or citizens of the Arab and Jewish States. Immigration into, and residence within, the borders of the city for nationals of other States shall be controlled by the Governor under the directions of the Trusteeship Council.

9. *Relations with the Arab and Jewish States.* Representatives of the Arab and Jewish States shall be accredited to the Governor of the City and charged with the protection of the interests of their States and nationals in connexion with the international administration of the City.

10. *Official languages.* Arabic and Hebrew shall be the official languages of the city. This will not preclude the adoption of one or more additional working languages, as may be required.

11. *Citizenship.* All the residents shall become *ipso facto* citizens of the City of Jerusalem unless they opt for citizenship of the State of which they have been citizens or, if Arabs or Jews, have filed notice of intention to become citizens of the Arab or Jewish State respectively, according to part I, section B, paragraph 9 of this plan.

The Trusteeship Council shall make arrangements for consular protection of the citizens of the City outside its territory.

12. *Freedoms of citizens.* (*a*) Subject only to the requirements of public order and morals, the inhabitants of the City shall be ensured the enjoyment of human rights and fundamental freedoms, including freedom of conscience, religion and worship, language, education, speech and Press, assembly and association, and petition.

(*b*) No discrimination of any kind shall be made between the inhabitants on the grounds of race, religion, language or sex.

(*c*) All persons within the City shall be entitled to equal protection of the laws.

[126]

(*d*) The family law and personal status of the various persons and communities and their religious interests, including endowments, shall be respected.

(*e*) Except as may be required for the maintenance of public order and good government, no measure shall be taken to obstruct or interfere with the enterprise of religious or charitable bodies of all faiths or to discriminate against any representative or member of these bodies on the ground of his religion or nationality.

(*f*) The City shall ensure adequate primary and secondary education for the Arab and Jewish communities respectively, in their own languages and in accordance with their cultural traditions.

The right of each community to maintain its own schools for the education of its own members in its own language, while conforming to such educational requirements of a general nature as the City may impose, shall not be denied or impaired. Foreign educational establishments shall continue their activity on the basis of their existing rights.

(*g*) No restriction shall be imposed on the free use by any inhabitant of the City of any language in private intercourse, in commerce, in religion, in the Press or in publications of any kind, or at public meetings.

13. *Holy Places.* (*a*) Existing rights in respect of Holy Places and religious buildings or sites shall not be denied or impaired.

(*b*) Free access to the Holy Places and religious buildings or sites and the free exercise of worship shall be secured in conformity with existing rights and subject to the requirements of public order and decorum.

(*c*) Holy Places and religious buildings or sites shall be preserved. No act shall be permitted which may in any way impair their sacred character. If at any time it appears to the Governor that any particular Holy Place, religious building or site is in need of urgent repair, the Governor may call upon the community or communities concerned to carry out such repair. The Governor may carry it out himself at the expense of the community or communities concerned if no action is taken within a reasonable time.

(*d*) No taxation shall be levied in respect of any Holy Place, religious building or site which was exempt from taxation on the date of the creation of the City. No change in the incidence of such taxation shall be made which would either discriminate between the owners or occupiers of Holy Places, religious buildings or sites, or would place such owners or occupiers in a position less favourable in relation to the general incidence of taxation than existed at the time of the adoption of the Assembly's recommendations.

14. *Special powers of the Governor in respect of the Holy Places, religious buildings and sites in the City and in any part of Palestine.* (*a*) The protection of the Holy Places, religious buildings and sites located in the City of Jerusalem shall be a special concern of the Governor.

(*b*) With relation to such places, buildings and sites in Palestine outside the city, the Governor shall determine, on the ground of powers granted to him by the Constitutions of both States, whether the provisions of the Constitutions of the Arab and Jewish States in Palestine dealing therewith and the religious rights appertaining thereto are being properly applied and respected.

(*c*) The Governor shall also be empowered to make decisions on the basis of existing rights in cases of disputes which may arise between the different religious communities or the rites of a religious community in respect of the Holy Places, religious buildings and sites in any part of Palestine.

In this task he may be assisted by a consultative council of representatives of different denominations acting in an advisory capacity.

D. Duration of the Special Regime

The Statute elaborated by the Trusteeship Council on the aforementioned principles shall come into force not later than 1 October 1948. It shall remain in force in the first instance for a period of ten years, unless the Trusteeship Council finds it necessary to undertake a re-examination of these provisions at an earlier date. After the expiration of this period the whole scheme shall be subject to re-examination by the Trusteeship Council in the light of the experience acquired with its functioning. The residents of the City shall be then free to express by means of a referendum their wishes as to possible modifications of the regime of the City.

PART IV.—CAPITULATIONS

States whose nationals have in the past enjoyed in Palestine the privileges and immunities of foreigners, including the benefits of consular jurisdiction and protection, as formerly enjoyed by capitulation or usage in the Ottoman Empire, are invited to renounce any right pertaining to them to the re-establishment of such privileges and immunities in the proposed Arab and Jewish States and the City of Jerusalem.

The Trusteeship Council's Draft Statute for Jerusalem
(March 28, 1950)

Preamble

WHEREAS the General Assembly of the United Nations in its Resolution 181 (II) of 29 November 1947, laid down that the City of Jerusalem, as delimited in that resolution, should be established as a *corpus separatum* under a Special International Regime and should be administered by the United Nations:

WHEREAS the General Assembly designated the Trusteeship Council to discharge the responsibilities of the Administering Authority on behalf of the United Nations:

WHEREAS the special objectives to be pursued by the United Nations in discharging its administrative obligations were set forth in the aforesaid Resolution as follows:

"(a) To protect and to preserve the unique spiritual and religious interests located in the City of the three great monotheistic faiths throughout the world, Christian, Jewish and Moslem; to this end to ensure that order and peace, and especially religious peace, reign in Jerusalem;

"(b) To foster cooperation among all the inhabitants of the City in their own interests as well as in order to encourage and support the peaceful development of the mutual relations between the two Palestinian peoples throughout the Holy Land; to promote the security, well-being and any constructive measures of development of the residents, having regard to the special circumstances and customs of the various peoples and communities":

WHEREAS the General Assembly in the aforesaid Resolution directed the Trusteeship Council to elaborate and approve a detailed Statute for the City and prescribed certain provisions, the substance of which should be contained therein:

WHEREAS the Trusteeship Council prepared on 21 April 1948 the Draft Statute for the City of Jerusalem (Document T/118/Rev.2):

WHEREAS the General Assembly of the United Nations, in its Resolution 194 (III) of 11 December 1948 resolved that a special treatment separate from that accorded to the rest of Palestine should be accorded to the Jerusalem area and that it should be placed under effective United Nations control:

WHEREAS the General Assembly of the United Nations, in its Resolution 303 (IV) of 9 December 1949 restated its intention that Jerusalem should be placed under a permanent international regime, which should contain appropriate guarantees for the protection of the Holy Places, both within and outside Jerusalem, and requested the Trusteeship Council to complete the preparation of the Statute of Jerusalem (T/118/Rev.2), omitting those provisions which have become inapplicable and, without prejudice to the fundamental principles of the international regime for Jerusalem set forth in General Assembly Resolution 181 (II) of 29 November 1947 to introduce therein amendments in the direction of its greater democratization, to approve the Statute, and to proceed immediately with its implementation:

THE TRUSTEESHIP COUNCIL,

IN PURSUANCE OF the aforesaid Resolutions,

ADOPTS the present Statute for the City of Jerusalem.

Article 1
Special International Regime

The present Statute defines the Special International Regime for the City of Jerusalem and constitutes it as a *corpus separatum* under the administration of the United Nations.

Article 2
Definitions and interpretations

In this Statute unless the contrary is stated or the context otherwise requires:

(a) "City" means the territory of the *corpus separatum*;

(b) "Governor" means the Governor of the City, and includes, to the extent of his authority, any officer authorized by or in pursuance of this Statute to perform the functions of the Governor;

(c) "Instructions of the Trusteeship Council" means any instructions, whether of a general or special character, which are given by the Trusteeship Council in relation to the application of this Statute;

(d) Words importing the plural or the singular may be construed as referring to one person or matter or to more than one person or matter;

(e) When a duty is imposed or a power is conferred, the duty shall be performed and the power may be exercised from time to time as occasion requires;

(f) When a power is conferred to make any order, or to enact any legislation, or to give any instruction or direction, the power shall be construed as including a power to rescind, repeal, amend or vary the order, legislation, instruction or direction;

(g) When a duty is imposed or a power is conferred on the holder of an office, the duty shall be performed and the power may be exercised by the holder of the office or by a person duly appointed to act for him.

Article 3
Authority of the Statute

This Statute shall prevail in the City. No judicial decision shall conflict or interfere with its provisions, and no administrative act or legislative measure which conflicts or interferes with its provisions shall be valid.

Article 4
Boundaries of the territory of the City

1. The territory of the City shall include the municipality of Jerusalem, as delimited on 29 November 1947, together with the surrounding villages and towns, the most eastern of which is Abu Dis; the most southern Bethlehem; the most western Ein Karim (including also the built-up area of Motsa) and the most northern Shu'fat.

2. The precise boundaries of the City shall be delimited on the ground, by a Commission to be nominated by the Trusteeship Council. A description of the boundaries so delimited shall be transmitted to the Trusteeship Council for its approval and a description of the approved boundaries shall be annexed to this Statute.

Article 5
Functions of the Trusteeship Council

The Trusteeship Council, by virtue of the authority conferred upon it by General Assembly resolutions 181 (II) of 29 November 1947 and 303 (IV) of 9 December 1949, shall discharge the responsibilities of the United Nations for the administration of the City in accordance with this Statute.

Article 6
Territorial integrity

1. The territorial integrity of the City and the special regime as defined in this Statute shall be assured by the United Nations.

2. The Governor, appointed by the Trusteeship Council in accordance with the provisions of Article 12, shall inform the Trusteeship Council of any situation relating to the City the continuance of which is likely to endanger the territorial integrity of the City, or of any threat of aggression or act of aggression against the City, or of any other attempt to alter by force the special regime as defined in the Statute. If the Trusteeship Council is not in session and the Governor considers that any of the foregoing contingencies is of such urgency as to require immediate action by the United Nations, he shall bring the matter to the immediate attention of the Security Council through the Secretary-General of the United Nations.

Article 7
Demilitarization and neutrality

1. The City shall be, and remain, neutral and inviolable.

2. The City shall be demilitarized and no para-military for-

mations, exercises or activities shall be permitted within its borders. No armed forces, except as may be provided under Article 15 of this Statute or under the authority of the Security Council, shall be allowed in the City.

Article 8
Flag, seal and coat of arms

The Legislative Council, constituted in accordance with the provisions of Article 21, may approve a flag, a seal and a coat of arms for the City.

Article 9
Human rights and fundamental freedoms

1. All persons are entitled to all the rights and freedoms set forth in this Statute, without distinction of any kind, such as race, colour, sex, language, religion, political, or other opinion, national or social origin, property, birth or other status.

2. All persons shall enjoy freedom of conscience and shall, subject only to the requirements of good government, public order, public morals and public health, enjoy all other human rights and fundamental freedoms, including freedom of religion and worship, language, education, speech and Press, assembly and association, petition (including petition to the Trusteeship Council) and migration and movement.

3. All persons have the right to life, liberty and security of person.

4. All persons are equal before the law and are entitled without any discrimination to equal protection of the law. All persons are entitled to equal protection against any discrimination in violation of this Statute and against any incitement to such discrimination.

5. No person may be arrested, detained, convicted or punished, except according to due process of law.

6. No person or property shall be subject to search or seizure, except according to due process of law.

7. All persons are entitled in full equality to a fair and public hearing by an independent and impartial tribunal, in the

determination of their rights and obligations and of any criminal charge against them.

8. All persons charged with a penal offence have the right to be presumed innocent until proved guilty according to law in a public trial at which they have had all the guarantees necessary for their defence.

No person shall be held guilty of any penal offence on account of any act or omission which did not constitute a penal offence, under national or international law, at the time when it was committed. Nor shall a heavier penalty be imposed than the one that was applicable at the time the penal offence was committed.

9. No person shall be subjected to arbitrary interference with his privacy, family, home or correspondence, nor to attacks upon his honour and reputation. All persons have the right to the protection of the law against such interference or attacks.

10. All persons have the right to freedom of thought, conscience and religion; this right includes freedom to change their religion or belief, and freedom, either alone or in community with others, either in public or in private, to manifest their religion or belief in teaching, practice, worship and observance.

11. All persons have the right to freedom of opinion and expression; this right includes freedom to hold opinions without interference, and to seek, receive and impart information and ideas through any media.

12. The legislation of the City shall neither place nor recognize any restriction upon the free use by any person of any language in private intercourse, in religious matters, in commerce, in the Press or in publications of any kind, or at public meetings.

13. Except as may be required for the maintenance of good government, public order, public morals and public health, no measure shall be taken to obstruct or interfere with the enterprise of religious or charitable bodies of all faiths.

14. The family law and personal status of all persons and

communities and their religious interests, including endowments, shall be respected.

15. All persons, as members of society, have the right to social security and are entitled to the realization, through national effort and international cooperation and, in accordance with the organization and resources of the City, of the economic, social and cultural rights indispensable for their dignity and the free development of their personalities.

16. Without prejudice to the provisions of the preceding paragraphs, the Universal Declaration of Human Rights shall be accepted as a standard of achievement for the City.

17. At such time as the proposed United Nations Covenant of Human Rights shall come into force the provisions of that Covenant shall enter into force also in the City in accordance with the provisions of Article 37 of this Statute.

Article 10
Definition of residents

For the purposes of Articles 11, 21, 22 and 42 of this Statute, the following persons shall be deemed to be residents of the City:

(a) Persons who were ordinarily resident in the City on 29 November 1947 and have remained ordinarily so resident since that date;

(b) Persons ordinarily resident in the City on 29 November 1947, who, having left the City as refugees, subsequently return for the purpose of residing there;

(c) Persons who do not qualify as residents under paragraphs (a) or (b) of this Article but who, after 29 November 1947 have been ordinarily resident in the City for a continuous period of not less than three years, and have not ceased to be ordinarily so resident: Provided that the legislation of the City may make provision for the registration of persons ordinarily resident in the City, and that subject to such exceptions as are provided for in that legislation, persons shall be deemed not to be ordinarily resident in the City for the purposes of paragraphs (a), (b) and (c) of this Article during any period in which they are in default in complying with the requirements of the legislation as to registration.

Article 11
Citizenship

1. All persons who at the date of coming into force of this Statute are residents of the City within the meaning of Article 10 of this Statute shall become *ipso facto* citizens of the City: Provided that:

(a) All residents of the City who, at the date of coming into force of this Statute, are citizens of any State and who give notice in such manner and within such period as the Governor shall by order prescribe of their intention to retain the citizenship of that State shall not be deemed to be citizens of the City;

(b) Unless a wife gives notice on her own behalf within the period prescribed by order of the Governor, she shall be bound by the decision of her husband in either submitting or not submitting notice as prescribed by sub-paragraph (a) above;

(c) A notice given by a parent or legal guardian in accordance with the provisions of sub-paragraph (a) above shall bind his or her children of minor age of whom he or she has custody: Provided that such a minor, on attaining his majority, may opt for the citizenship of the City by giving notice in such manner as the Governor may by order prescribe.

2. Subject to the provisions of paragraph 1 of this Article, the conditions for the acquisition of citizenship of the City by persons who become residents after the date of the coming into force of this Statute and for the loss of citizenship of the City shall be laid down by the legislation of the City.

Article 12
Selection and term of office of
the Governor

1. The Governor shall be appointed by and responsible to the Trusteeship Council.

2. The term of office of the Governor shall be three years from the time of his appointment: Provided that:

(a) The Trusteeship Council may extend the term of office of the Governor in any particular case for such period as it may deem fit;

(b) The Governor may resign his appointment upon due notice to the Trusteeship Council, and the Trusteeship Council may terminate his appointment for due cause at any time.

3. At the expiration of his term of office, a Governor shall be eligible for re-appointment.

Article 13
General powers of the Governor

1. The Governor shall be the representative of the United Nations in the City.

2. The Governor, on behalf of the United Nations, shall exercise executive authority in the City and shall act as the chief administrative officer thereof, subject only to the provisions of this Statute and to the Instructions of the Trusteeship Council. He shall be responsible for ensuring the good government, public order, public morals and public health of the City in accordance with the special objectives set out in the Preamble to this Statute.

3. The Governor shall be responsible for exercising such supervision over religious or charitable bodies of all faiths in the City as may be required for the maintenance of good government, public order, public morals and public health. He shall exercise such supervision in conformity with existing rights and traditions.

4. The Governor and his official and private property shall not be in any way subject to the jurisdiction of the Legislative Council or of the Courts of the City.

Article 14
Power of pardon and reprieve

The Governor may grant to any offender convicted of any offence in any Court of the City a pardon, either free or conditional, or may grant any remission of the sentence passed on such offender, or any respite of the execution of such sentence, for such period as the Governor deems fit, and may remit any fines, penalties or forfeitures which may accrue or become payable to the City by virtue of the judgment of any Court of the City or of the operation of any legislation of the City.

Article 15
Preservation of order

1. The Governor shall be responsible for the organization and direction of the police forces necessary for the maintenance of internal law and order.

2. The Governor shall organize and direct a special police force, of such numbers as he may deem necessary, for the maintenance of internal law and order, and especially for the protection of the Holy Places, religious buildings and sites.

Article 16
Emergency powers of the Governor

1. If, in the opinion of the Governor, the administration is being seriously obstructed or prevented by the non-cooperation or interference of persons or groups of persons, the Governor, during the period of the emergency, shall take such measures and enact by order such legislation as he may deem necessary to restore the effective functioning of the administration, and such orders shall have effect notwithstanding anything to the contrary in any legislation in force.

2. The circumstances in which the Governor may have exercised any power conferred on him by this Article shall be reported to the Trusteeship Council as soon as may be practicable.

Article 17
Organization of the administration

1. The Governor shall be assisted by a Chief Secretary who shall be appointed by the Trusteeship Council on the recommendation of the Governor.

2. The Governor shall appoint an administrative staff, including an Attorney General, the members of which shall be selected on a non-discriminatory basis for their competence and integrity and, whenever practicable, from among the residents of the City. Subject to any instructions of the Trusteeship Council and to any legislation of the City, the appointments of members of the administrative staff may be terminated by the Governor at any time.

3. There shall be a Council of Administration consisting of the Chief Secretary and such other principal officers and residents as the Governor may appoint. The Governor may also, if he considers it desirable, add to the Council other persons chosen by him. The Council of Administration shall advise and assist the Governor in the administration of the City.

4. In the performance of their duties, the Governor, the members of the Council of Administration and administrative staff, including members of the police forces, shall not seek or receive any instructions from any Government or any authority other than the Government of the City or the Trusteeship Council.

Article 18
Disqualification from public office

A person shall be disqualified from holding any public office, central or local, in the City, including membership of the Council of Administration and of the Legislative Council, if he holds any office under any other Government: Provided that the Governor may appoint to any public office in the City for a limited period any person seconded from the service of another Government.

Article 19
Oaths of Office

The Governor, the Chief Secretary, members of the Judiciary, members of the Council of Administration, members of the Legislative Council, members of the special police force and

[140]

such other officers as the Governor may determine, shall take such oaths and make such affirmations as are specified in the Instructions of the Trusteeship Council.

Article 20
Acting Governor

If the office of Governor is vacant, or if the Governor is absent from the City or is unable to exercise his powers or perform his duties, the officer holding substantively the appointment of Chief Secretary, or, if there is no such officer or he is absent from the City or unable to act, such person as may have been authorized to act in the circumstances by the Instructions of the Trusteeship Council, may exercise all the powers and perform all the duties of the Governor so long as the office of Governor is vacant or the Governor is absent from the City or unable to exercise his powers or perform his duties.

Article 21
The Legislative Council

1. A Legislative Council, consisting of a single chamber, shall have power to legislate, consistent with the provisions of this Statute, upon all matters affecting the interests of the City, except such matters as are included within powers specifically granted by this Statute to the Trusteeship Council or to any other authority.

2. The Legislative Council shall be composed of citizens or residents of the City, twenty-five years of age and over, elected or designated in accordance with the provisions of this Article and of Article 22 of this Statute. The Trusteeship Council may determine any special conditions under which residents who are citizens of another State may be eligible for membership.

3. The Legislative Council shall consist of twenty-five elected members and a number of other members to be decided as hereinafter provided who shall be designated by the Heads of the principal religious communities.

The twenty-five members shall be elected by four electoral

colleges: Christian, Jewish, Moslem and mixed, the latter being composed of the residents of the City who declare that they do not wish to register with any of the other three colleges. The Governor shall make all the necessary arrangements for opening and keeping the electoral registers in each of these four colleges.

The first three colleges shall each elect eight members, and the fourth college shall elect one member, to the Legislative Council.

The other members of the Council shall be designated by the Heads of the principal religious communities of the City: the number of these members representing the Christian religion, the Jewish religion and the Moslem religion being equal. The Governor shall submit to the Trusteeship Council a plan for the allocation of the non-elective seats among the principal communities of each of the three religions.

4. The proceedings of the Legislative Council shall not be invalidated by reason of a vacancy in its membership.

5. The legislation of the City may make provisions as to disqualifications from election to and membership of the Legislative Council, resulting from loss of legal capacity.

6. The legislation of the City shall provide for the remuneration of the members of the Legislative Council.

Article 22
Elections to the Legislative Council

1. The elected members of the Legislative Council shall be elected by residents of the City, twenty-one years of age and over, irrespective of nationality or sex, on the basis of universal and secret suffrage and proportional representation in each electoral college. For this purpose every resident of the City may register with the college of his own community, or with the mixed college; he may be registered at only one college.

2. The legislation of the City shall provide for an electoral law and make provisions regarding disqualifications from voting, resulting from loss of legal capacity.

Article 23
Duration of the Legislative Council

1. The term of the Legislative Council shall be four years from the date of its election, unless it is earlier dissolved.

2. If, at the end of a four-year term of the Legislative Council, it is the opinion of the Governor that circumstances are inappropriate for the conduct of a general election, the Legislative Council may by legislation prolong the term for a further period not exceeding one year, provided that the Governor shall forthwith report the circumstances to the Trusteeship Council for instructions.

3. If, in the opinion of the Governor, the special objectives of this Statute are being gravely imperilled by the conduct of the Legislative Council, the Governor may suspend the Legislative Council for a maximum period of one month. A further suspension may not however be ordered during the same session without the consent of the Trusteeship Council.

Whenever the Governor has exercised his right of suspension he shall forthwith report the circumstances to the Trusteeship Council.

4. If a serious political crisis arises in the City and if, in the opinion of the Governor, the dissolution of the Legislative Council would be justified, he shall report the circumstances to the Trusteeship Council which may, after examining the Governor's report, order such dissolution, and at the same time fix a date for the holding of new elections.

Article 24
Legislation and resolutions

1. Bills and resolutions may be introduced in the Legislative Council by any member thereof.

2. The Governor, or a member of his staff designated by him, may make statements or answer questions before the Legislative Council or may introduce any bill or resolution and may participate without vote in the deliberations of the Legislative Council on the bill or resolution so introduced.

3. A bill adopted by the Legislative Council shall become

law only upon approval and promulgation by the Governor except that on the expiration of thirty days after the transmission of a bill to the Governor, if he has by that time neither approved nor disapproved it, he shall promulgate it as a law. The Governor may disapprove a bill, if, in his opinion, it is in conflict with the provisions of this Statute, or it would impede the administration of the City or inflict undue hardship on any section of the inhabitants of the City, and he shall then inform both the Legislative Council and the Trusteeship Council of the reasons for his disapproval.

Article 25
Legislation by order of the Governor

1. At any time when there is no Legislative Council or the Legislative Council is suspended, the Governor may legislate by order and any such order shall become law. Such order shall be laid before the Legislative Council as soon as may be practicable and shall remain law until and unless repealed or amended by the Legislative Council in accordance with the provisions of paragraph 3 of Article 24.

2. When the Legislative Council is in session but fails to adopt in time a bill deemed essential to the normal functioning of the Administration the Governor may make temporary orders.

3. The Governor shall forthwith report to the Trusteeship Council any action taken by him in accordance with the provisions of this article and shall comply with the Instructions of the Trusteeship Council given in relation thereto.

Article 26
Standing Orders of the Legislative Council

1. The Legislative Council shall adopt such Standing Orders for the conduct of its business, including the election of a President, (who may or may not be a member of the Legislative Council), as it may deem appropriate.

2. The Governor shall convene the first session of each Legislative Council and may at any time convene an extraordinary session.

3. Subject to the provisions of Article 23 of this Statute, subsequent sessions of the Legislative Council shall be convened in accordance with the Standing Orders of the Legislative Council.

4. Subject to the provisions of Article 23 of this Statute, the Governor shall convene an extraordinary session of the Legislative Council upon the request of a majority of the members.

5. A majority of the members of the Legislative Council shall form a quorum.

6. Decisions of the Legislative Council shall be taken by a simple majority of those present and voting. Members who abstain from voting shall not be counted as voting.

Article 27
Immunity of members of the Legislative Council

1. No member of the Legislative Council shall be liable to any judicial or administrative penalty, or be called to account in any other way outside the Legislative Council, by reason of anything which he may have said, or of any vote which he may have cast, in the course of his duties as a member of the Legislative Council.

2. No member of the Legislative Council shall be liable during the sessions of the Council in criminal, administrative or disciplinary proceedings, nor shall he be deprived of his liberty, without the permission of the Legislative Council: Provided that he may be apprehended in the act of committing a crime and detained if his detention is or becomes imperative in the interests of justice, but in any such case his apprehension shall be reported as soon as may be practicable to the Legislative Council and he shall be released without delay should the Legislative Council so request.

Article 28
Judicial system

1. The legislation of the City shall provide for an independent judicial system for the City, including a Supreme Court and such subordinate and other Courts as may be deemed ap-

propriate. Such legislation shall establish the jurisdiction of the Courts and provide for their organization.

2. All persons shall be subject to the jurisdiction of the City, subject to any immunity for which provision is made in this Statute.

3. The Supreme Court shall consist of such number of Judges, not being less than three or more than five as the Trusteeship Council may determine, of whom one shall be President of the Supreme Court and shall be styled Chief Justice. They shall be appointed by, and their appointments shall be terminated only by, the Trusteeship Council.

4. Judicial personnel other than the Chief Justice and the Judges of the Supreme Court shall be appointed by and may be suspended or dismissed by the Chief Justice with the approval of the Governor, in accordance with any procedure for which provision may be made in the Instructions of the Trusteeship Council.

5. Subject to the special objectives set out in the Preamble to this Statute and to social evolution in the City, the existing status and jurisdiction of religious Courts in the City shall be respected. In the case of any conflict regarding jurisdiction between religious Courts or between religious Courts and civil Courts, the Supreme Court shall consider the case and decide in which Court the jurisdiction shall lie.

6. Decisions by the Supreme Court shall be made by a majority of its members: Provided that, if in any case the opinion of the Court be equally divided, the opinion of the Chief Justice shall prevail.

Article 29
Constitutionality of legislation and administrative acts

1. In cases brought before the Courts of the City this Statute shall prevail over any legislation or administrative act. The Supreme Court shall have original and appellate jurisdiction in all cases involving claims that such legislation or act is incompatible with the provisions of this Statute.

2. In any case in which the Supreme Court decides that any legislation or administrative act is incompatible with the provisions of this Statute, such legislation or administrative act shall be void and of no effect.

Article 30
Access to the City

1. Subject only to the requirements of good government, public order, public morals and public health:

(a) Freedom of entry into and of temporary residence in and of exit from the City shall be ensured to all foreign pilgrims and visitors without distinction as to nationality or faith;

(b) The legislation of the City shall make special provisions to facilitate entry and exit from the City for inhabitants of adjoining areas.

2. Immigration into the City for the purposes of residence shall be controlled by order of the Governor under the Instructions of the Trusteeship Council having regard to the absorptive capacity of the City and the maintenance of equality between the various communities.

Article 31
Official and working languages

Arabic and Hebrew shall be the official and working languages of the City. The legislation of the City may adopt one or more additional working languages as may be required.

Article 32
Educational system and cultural and benevolent institutions

1. All persons have a right to education. Education shall be directed to the full physical, intellectual, moral and spiritual development of the human personality and to the strengthening of respect for human rights and fundamental freedoms. It shall be directed to the promotion of understanding, tolerance and friendship among all national, racial and religious groups. It shall in particular be directed to the furtherance of the ac-

tivities of the United Nations, to the establishment of peace and to the attainment of the special objectives set out in the Preamble to this Statute.

2. Education, in its elementary stages, shall be free and compulsory. In its secondary stages, it shall insofar as may be practicable be free. Technical and professional educational facilities shall be provided insofar as may be practicable and those supported by public funds shall be equally accessible to all on the basis of merit.

3. The City shall maintain or subsidize and supervise a system of primary and secondary education on an equitable basis for all communities in their respective languages and in accordance with their respective cultural traditions: Provided that such communities have a sufficient number of pupils to justify a separate school.

4. Subject to the provisions of paragraph 1 of this Article and to such educational requirements of a general nature as the legislation of the City may impose, any community or any specific group within any community may maintain its own institutions for the education of its own members in its own language according to its own cultural traditions.

5. Subject to the provisions of paragraph 1 of this Article and to the legislation of the City, private or foreign educational establishments may be maintained in the City: Provided that existing rights shall continue unimpaired.

6. Educational and cultural establishments, charitable institutions and hospitals already in existence or founded after the coming into force of this Statute shall enjoy the fiscal privileges provided for in paragraph 6 of Article 38.

7. At the request of a parent or legal guardian, any child may be exempted from religious instruction in any school supported in whole or in part by public funds.

Article 33
Broadcasting and television

1. Radio broadcasting and television shall be reserved to the City administration and shall be controlled by a Joint Broad-

casting Council, which shall be appointed by and shall be responsible to the Governor and which shall include an equal number of representatives of each of the three principal religions: Christian, Jewish and Moslem.

2. Representatives of the Christian, Jewish and Moslem religions shall have equal opportunities of access to the broadcasting and television facilities of the City.

3. The principle of freedom of expression shall apply to broadcasting, but it shall be the responsibility of the Joint Broadcasting Council to ensure that the radio is used to further the interests of peace and mutual understanding between the inhabitants of the City and of the objectives of this Statute and of the Charter of the United Nations.

Article 34
Economic provisions

1. The plan for the economic and financial organization of the City adopted by the Trusteeship Council in accordance with the provisions of paragraph 4 of Article 43 shall form an Annex to this Statute.

2. In the economic and social fields the rights and interests of the inhabitants shall be considered as of primary importance. Subject to this provision, all economic, industrial and commercial matters shall be regulated on the basis of equal treatment and non-discrimination for all States, nationals, and companies or associations controlled by their nationals; and an equal treatment and non-discrimination shall be ensured in respect of freedom of transit, including transit and navigation by air, acquisition of property, both movable and immovable, protection of persons and property and the exercise of professions and trades.

Article 35
Budgets

1. The Governor shall be responsible for the preparation of the annual and supplementary budgets of the City; and only

the Governor or a member of his staff designated by him shall introduce budgets in the Legislative Council.

2. The financial provision made by the Governor in the budgets for the maintenance of the special police force shall not be altered by the Legislative Council. The Trusteeship Council may determine other services for which the financial provision made by the Governor in the budgets shall not be altered by the Legislative Council.

3. The Governor may authorise, in anticipation of approval by the Legislative Council, expenditure for which there is no provision in the budgets, if in his opinion such expenditure becomes a matter of urgency.

Article 36
Local Autonomy

1. Existing local autonomous units and such new local autonomous units as may be created shall enjoy wide powers of local government and administration in accordance with the legislation of the City.

2. The plan for local autonomy adopted by the Trusteeship Council in accordance with the provisions of paragraph 5 of Article 43 shall form an Annex to this Statute.

Article 37
External affairs

1. Subject to the provisions of this Statute, and to the Instructions of the Trusteeship Council, the Governor shall conduct the external affairs of the City.

2. The Governor may ensure by means of special international agreements or otherwise the protection abroad of the interests of the City and of its citizens.

3. The Governor may accredit representatives to foreign States for the protection of the interests of the City and its citizens in those States.

4. Representatives may be accredited to the Governor by any State if he so permits.

5. The Governor, on behalf of the City, may sign treaties

which are consistent with this Statute, and shall adhere to the provisions of any international conventions and recommendations drawn up by the United Nations or by the Specialized Agencies referred to in Article 57 of the Charter of the United Nations which may be appropriate to the particular circumstances of the City, or would conduce to the achievement of the special objectives set out in the Preamble to this Statute.

6. Such treaties and international undertakings entered into by the Governor shall be submitted for ratification to the Legislative Council. If the Legislative Council does not ratify any such treaties or international undertakings within six months of the date of signature by the Governor, the matter shall be referred to the Trusteeship Council which shall have the power to ratify them.

7. Foreign Powers shall enjoy immunities no less than those in force on 29 November 1947 in respect of their property within the City.

Article 38
Holy Places, religious buildings and sites

1. The protection of Holy Places, religious buildings and sites shall be the special concern of the Governor.

2. If any question arises as to whether any place, building or site not hitherto regarded as a Holy Place, religious building or site shall be a Holy Place, religious building or site for the purpose of this Statute, the Governor shall decide. For the purpose of deciding any such question, the Governor may appoint a Committee of Enquiry to assist him.

3. If any dispute arises between different religious communities or between different confessions and faiths in connection with any Holy Place, religious building or site, the Governor shall decide on the basis of existing rights. For the purpose of deciding any such dispute, the Governor may appoint a Committee of Enquiry to assist him. He may also, if he shall deem fit, be assisted by a consultative council of representatives of different denominations acting in an advisory capacity.

4. In questions of law an appeal shall lie to the Supreme

Court from any decision of the Governor taken in accordance with the provisions of paragraphs 2 or 3 of this Article.

5. If at any time it appears to the Governor that any Holy Place, religious building or site is in need of urgent repairs, he may call upon the community or denomination or section of the community concerned to carry out such repairs. If the repairs are not carried out, or are not completed within a reasonable time, the Governor may arrange for repairs to be carried out or completed and the expenses of so doing shall be a charge on the revenues of the City but may be recovered from the community or denomination or section of the community concerned, subject to existing rights.

6. No form of taxation shall be levied in respect of any Holy Place, religious building or site which was exempt from taxation of that form on 29 November 1947. No change in the incidence of any form of taxation shall be made which would either discriminate between the owners or occupiers of Holy Places, religious buildings and sites or would place such owners or occupiers in a position less favourable in relation to the general incidence of that form of taxation than existed on 29 November 1947.

7. The Governor shall ensure that the property rights of churches, missions and other religious or charitable agencies shall be confirmed and respected. He shall ensure, further, that all such property which, since the outbreak of the Second World War had been seized without equitable compensation but which has not already been returned or for one reason or another could not be returned to its original owners, shall either be restored to them or be transferred to another church, or mission or other religious or charitable agency, representative of the same confession.

8. The Governor shall by order ensure that:

(a) His decisions taken in accordance with the provisions of paragraphs 2 and 3 of this Article are carried into effect and that provision is made for the recovery of sums recoverable in accordance with the provisions of paragraph 5 of this Article;

(b) Existing rights in respect of Holy Places, religious buildings and sites shall not be denied or impaired;

(c) Subject to the requirements of good government, public order, public morals and public health, free access is maintained to Holy Places, religious buildings and sites and that free exercise or worship therein is secured in conformity with existing rights;

(d) Holy Places, religious buildings and sites are preserved;

(e) No act is committed which may in any way impair the sacred character of Holy Places, religious buildings or sites;

(f) Provisions of this Article generally, and the special objectives set out in the Preamble to this Statute insofar as they relate to Holy Places, religious buildings and sites, are carried into effect.

9. An order made in accordance with the provisions of paragraph 8 of this Article may contain penal provisions and shall have effect notwithstanding anything to the contrary in any legislation.

10. The Governor shall transmit a copy of every order made in accordance with the provisions of paragraph 8 of this Article to the Trusteeship Council as soon as may be practicable and the Trusteeship Council may give such instructions to the Governor in relation thereto as it may deem fit.

Article 39
Protection of antiquities

Legislation of the City shall provide for the protection of antiquities.

Article 40
Capitulations

Foreign Powers whose nationals have in the past enjoyed in the City the privileges and immunities of foreigners, including the benefits of consular jurisdiction and protection as formerly enjoyed by capitulation or usage in the Ottoman Empire, are invited to renounce, if they have not already renounced, any right pertaining to them as regards the re-establishment of such privileges and immunities in the City. Any privileges and immunities which may be retained, shall be respected.

Article 41
Entry into force of the Statute

This Statute shall come into force at a date to be determined by a resolution of the Trusteeship Council.

Article 42
Re-examination of the Statute

1. This Statute shall remain in force in the first instance for a period of ten years, unless the Trusteeship Council amends it before the expiration of this period.

2. On the expiration of this period of ten years, the whole Statute shall be subject to re-examination by the Trusteeship Council. The residents of the City shall then be free to express by means of a referendum their wishes as to possible modifications of the regime of the City. The Trusteeship Council shall in due course lay down the procedure by which this referendum shall be conducted.

Article 43
Transitory provisions

1. *Flag*

Unless the Legislature of the City decides otherwise, the flag of the United Nations shall be flown from official buildings.

2. *First elections to the Legislative Council*

The first elections of members to the Legislative Council shall be held as soon as possible after the entry into force of this Statute at such date and in such manner as shall be provided by order of the Governor, in accordance with the provisions of Articles 21 and 22 of this Statute and of the Instructions of the Trusteeship Council.

3. *Provisional President of the Legislative Council*

The Provisional President of the Legislative Council shall be appointed by the Governor and shall remain in office until the election of a President by the Legislative Council.

4. *Economic provisions*

The Governor shall take prompt steps to formulate, with the advice and help of such experts as may seem to him desirable, the economic and financial principles upon which the Government of the City is to be based. In doing so he shall take into consideration the desirability of meeting the costs of the administration of the City from rates, taxes and other local revenues, and the possibility that any advances from the United Nations towards such expenditure will be in the form of loans. The Governor, within six months of the date of his appointment, shall submit to the Trusteeship Council for its consideration a plan for the economic and financial organization of the City.

Pending a decision by the Trusteeship Council in this matter, the Governor may temporarily take such economic and financial measures as he may deem necessary for the proper administration of the City.

Commercial concessions, or concessions in respect of public services, granted in the city prior to 29 November 1947 shall continue to be valid according to their terms, unless modified by agreement between the Governor and the concession holder.

5. *Local autonomy*

The Governor, after consultation with the Legislative Council and, if possible, within six months of the date of his appointment, shall submit to the Trusteeship Council for its consideration a plan for dividing the City into local autonomous units and for the allocation of powers between the City authorities and the authorities of those autonomous units.

6. *Continuity of legislation*

The legislation in force in the City on the day preceding the termination of the Mandate, insofar as it is not inconsistent with the provisions of this Statute, shall be applicable in the City until such time as it may be amended or repealed by legislation of the City.

7. *Refugees*

Having regard to any decisions or recommendations which

have been, or may be, made by organs of the United Nations or to any agreement which have been accordingly concluded between the States concerned regarding the problem of the Palestine refugees, the Governor of the City, as soon as this Statute enters into force, shall facilitate the repatriation, re-settlement and economic and social rehabilitation of persons who, on 29 November 1947, were ordinarily resident in the City and have left the City as refugees, as well as the payment of any indemnities which may be due to them.

The Security Council's Resolution
(November 22, 1967)

The Security Council,

Expressing its continued concern with the grave situation in the Middle East,

Emphasizing the inadmissibility of the acquisition of territory by war and the need to work for a just and lasting peace in which every State in the area can live in security,

Emphasizing further that all Member States in their acceptance of the Charter of the United Nations have undertaken a commitment to act in accordance with Article 2 of the Charter,

1. *Affirms* that the fulfilment of Charter principles requires the establishment of a just and lasting peace in the Middle East which should include the application of both the following principles:

i) Withdrawal of Israel armed forces from territories occupied in the recent conflict;

ii) Termination of all claims or states of belligerency and respect for and acknowledgement of the sovereignty, territorial integrity and political independence of every State in the area and their right to live in peace within secure and recognized boundaries free from threats or acts of force;

2. *Affirms further* the necessity

(a) For guaranteeing freedom of navigation through international waterways in the area;

(b) For achieving a just settlement of the refugee problem;

(c) For guaranteeing the territorial inviolability and political independence of every State in the area, through measures including the establishment of demilitarized zones;

3. *Requests* the Secretary-General to designate a Special Representative to proceed to the Middle East to establish and maintian contacts with the States concerned in order to promote agreement and assist efforts to achieve a peaceful and accepted settlement in accordance with the provisions and principles in this resolution;

[157]

4. *Requests* the Secretary-General to report to the Security Council on the progress of the efforts of the Special Representative as soon as possible.

Adopted unanimously at the 1382nd meeting.

INDEX

Abdullah, Emir, 45
Al Fatah, 12-13, 44
Allenby, Edmund Henry
  Hynman, 6
anti-Zionism, 37-38, 62
Aqaba, Straits of, 17n
Arab League, 17n, 19
Arab Legion, 71
Arab Palestinian State, 7-8,
  47, 50-51
Arab socialism, 62
Arafat, Yasir, 13
armistices, 8
arms race, 24-25; in chemical
  and gas weapons, 18; in
  nuclear weapons, 17-18, 24

Ba'ath, 62
"behavior control," 11
Bentham, Jeremy, 55
"binding advisory opinion,"
  78-79

chemical and gas weapons, 18
Churchill, Winston, 45
commandos, *see* Palestinian
  commandos

Druze, 63, 65; Golan Heights
  as trust territory for, 66-70;
  self-determination of, 65-66,
  68-70

Egypt, 8, 23, 28, 29, 44;
  militarism of, 23-25; and
  Sinai, 23-43
ethnic identification, 63-64
ethnic nationalism, 81

Faisal, 45
Farouk, 23
"fate control," 11
Four Power Conference, 10,
  77, 79
France, 8
"Free Officers," 8

Galili, Israel, 54-56
Gaza, 8, 47
General Assembly's Resolution
  on the Future Government
  of Palestine, 100-101
Golan Heights, 61-70
Great Britain, 5-6, 8, 45; as
  Mandatory, 7, 46
guerrilla warfare, *see*
  Palestinian commandos

Hashemite Kingdom of Jordan,
  see Arab Palestinian State
Hourani, Cecil, 38
Hussein, 50, 52, 53

"imposed" solutions, 20-21
"indigenous" solutions, 20-21
International Atomic Energy
  Agency, 32
International Bank for
  Reconstruction and
  Development, 30, 32-33,
  40-42
International Court of Justice,
  32, 78-79
International Labour
  Organization, 32
International Monetary Fund,
  30

[159]